# SALTWATER
# GAME FISH
## OF NORTH AMERICA

# SALTWATER
# GAME FISH
## OF NORTH AMERICA

Herbert A. Schaffner

FRIEDMAN/FAIRFAX
PUBLISHERS

**A FRIEDMAN/FAIRFAX BOOK**

© 1995 by Michael Friedman Publishing Group, Inc.

**Library of Congress Cataloging-in-Publication Data**

Schaffner, Herbert A.
    Saltwater game fish of North America / Herbert A. Schaffner.
        p.   cm.
    Includes index.
    ISBN 1-56799-158-0 (pbk.)
    1. Saltwater fishing—North America.   2. Marine fishes—North
America.  I. Title.
SH462.S34  1995
799.1'6—dc20
                                      94-27974
                                          CIP

Editor: Sharyn Rosart
Art Director: Robert W. Kosturko
Designer: Devorah Levinrad
Layout: Deborah Kaplan
Photography Editor: Christopher C. Bain
Photography Researcher: Ede Rothaus

All illustrations are by Ron Pittard © Windsor Publications, Inc., Eugene, Oregon

Typeset by Mar + X Myles
Color separations by Universal Color Scanning, Ltd.
Printed in China by Leefung-Asco Printers Ltd.

For bulk purchases and special sales, please contact:
Friedman/Fairfax Publishers
Attention: Sales Department
15 West 26th Street
New York, NY 10010
212/685-6610  FAX 212/685-1307

# $A$cknowledgments

While I have much more to learn about the piscine universe, I would know even less without
the guidance of my father, who made me a fisherman. Thanks, Dad. The companionship
of many angling friends through the years was essential to my maturing
angling abilities and enjoyment of the sport.

I must thank Tim Frew and Sharyn Rosart of the Michael Friedman Publishing Group. Tim
got the project rolling with the right mixture of humor and enthusiasm. Sharyn Rosart
carefully guided the book to completion with encouragement and efficiency. She showed a
nice sense of humor, too. Devorah Levinrad was a pleasure to work with, and learned quickly
about fish and fish photography. Best of luck to them all.

Thanks from the heart to Laura Schenone, my wife, for computer time—and everything.

This book is dedicated to Andy McCormick, a good friend and very good writer.

**Introduction to Saltwater Game Fish**

# PART 1

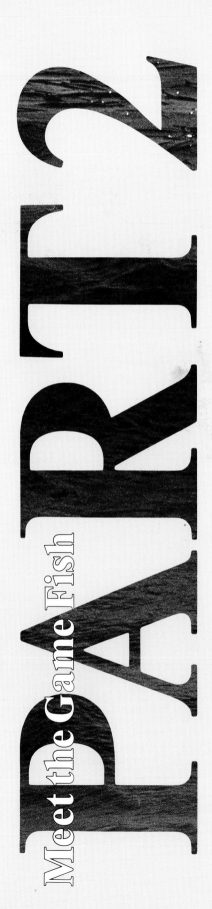

**PART 2**

**Meet the Game Fish**

'Wouldst thou'-so the helmsman answered-

'Learn the secrets of the sea?

Only those who brave its danger

Comprehend its mystery!'

–Longfellow

# Introduction

Whether you fish, scuba or skin dive, boat or sail, *Saltwater Game Fish of North America* will expand and enrich your experience in the oceans. The fish of the sea are not only exciting and interesting to watch and catch, but they are also the most visible elements in a dizzyingly complex ecosystem, alive with over twenty thousand different saltwater fish species, and thousands more species of crustacea, invertebrates, mammals, and planktons. Much can be learned about the secrets of the sea from its not-very-secretive piscine inhabitants. Early man's primitive drawings and stories of fish on cave walls, the numerous leading parts fish have played in ancient myths and religions, and their vital role in the diets of early coastal peoples bear out their crucial symbolic and practical significance in human affairs from the earliest stages.

This book is intended not only to enliven your interest in the mysterious sea, but also to provide a set of informational "flash cards" to establish familiarity with major game-fish species and erect signposts for further study and research, and, best of all, to help you catch more fish in salt water.

The ocean covers almost seventy percent of the globe and contains 330 million cubic feet of water. It is deep enough to swallow mountains and large enough to cover entire continents. The vastness and depth of the ocean and its life both intimidate and thrill the angler or explorer. It is as unknown in many parts as the planets. It is contoured by hidden topographies of reefs and ridges, shelves and drop-offs, grassy flats, terrifyingly deep banks and precipitous cliffs. Its creatures are influenced by profound invisible forces—oceanic currents, sheets of ice, massive tides, the absence or overabundance of food. To subdue a creature that participates in such vast natural complexity is to gain a part of that ancient complexity for oneself.

*Saltwater Game Fish of North America* will show how the various behaviors (mating, migration, feeding) of underwater wildlife intersect in a complex web of interdependent relationships. Fish are sport to the angler, but *they* don't know that. To the fish, their environment is the entire universe, and our interference makes no sense except that our presence is disturbing or frightening to them.

*Saltwater Game Fish of North America* is also supremely practical. Every game fish entry provides basic, useful information to make your angling and sporting efforts more productive and enjoyable. Each species entry provides the information necessary to identify fish through color, size, and unique species characteristics, including fin location, gill and scale counts, and jaw and tooth configurations. Also included are descriptions of how big each variety of fish usually gets, and the world records for size. Each entry also explains the important migratory, spawning, and feeding habits of the ocean's game fish, plus the best angling methods to attract and catch them. These thumbnail sketches may spur your own private research projects.

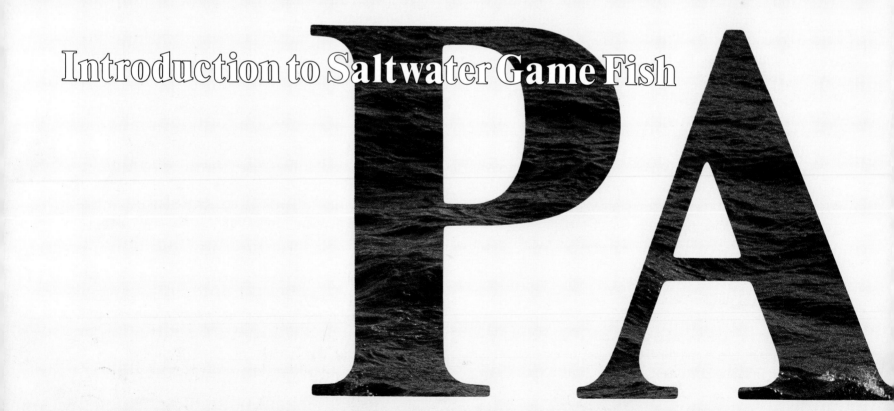

# Introduction to Saltwater Game Fish

PA

# The Fragile Bounty of the Sea

The earth's oceans are vast. Anyone who has traveled them must wonder how any fish resource could become depleted; it seems that a million commercial trawlers couldn't make a dent. Yet wherever commercial fisheries have discovered large numbers of salable food fish, they have relentlessly harvested them. The sea's fish are vital to the food markets of the world. Millions and millions of dollars are spent every year harvesting the "limitless" crops of the sea. Yet in comparison to the sophisticated cycling, irrigating, and resource-preservation tactics of land agriculture, industrial fisheries follow few similar strategies in conserving or rotating their "crops" in order to provide for the future.

While relatively few game-fish species are pursued by saltwater anglers, they number far more than freshwater game fish and are of greater importance to world food markets. Unfortunately, ecological history shows that sport fishing has also played a devastating role in depleting populations of valuable game fish.

Although they are often opposed to commercial fishing interests, sport fishers must understand in general terms how even light sport-fishing pressure applied to an individual feeding ground over a long period of time can affect the reproductive future of game-fish species and the balance of life in an oceanic habitat. "Keepers" are inevitably the larger, breeding-age adults that propagate the species season after season and feed on the middle-level predators that eat enormous numbers of their own hatched fingerlings and fry.

To ignore this issue is to threaten the future of one's own sport: If it were discovered tomorrow that a limited supply of baseballs existed (and once depleted this supply could not be replenished), major league teams would, of course, husband their supplies carefully. Too often, saltwater anglers have viewed their prey as part of an inexhaustible vein of progeny always available for their pleasure; the histories of game fish such as the salmon, striped bass, cod, and bluefish offer stark contradiction. As a result, species

preservation and management is now a significant influence in the federal regulation of saltwater sport fishing.

Sport-fishing associations and representatives claim with some justification that their sport generates a great deal of tourist revenue for motel and restaurant owners, charter captains, and other members of seaside fishing towns, while exerting a fraction of the commercial fisheries' pressure on food-fish species. Yet anglers suffer regulation in similar proportion to commercial fishers. The angling history of the Atlantic salmon, with its drastic slump in post-grilse (one-year-at-sea) adults during the past seven to ten years, reflected the tremendous surge in commercial salmon netting off the coasts of Greenland and Iceland, and the thousands of salmon caught in Canadian tidal gill nets. However, Canadian sport fishermen were restricted as much as the netters. Intense lobbying by Canadian sportsmen and women and conservation groups have now forced the Canadian government to target policy at netters first and anglers second. A recent government buyout of commercial fishing licenses has had a clear and positive impact on runs of salmon in Canada. The U.S. has made it illegal for "any vessel of the United States" to catch or land any Atlantic salmon from the ocean. Any incidental catches of the Atlantic salmon "must be released in such a manner as to insure maximum probability of survival," according to U.S. regulations. Any sport or commercial fisherman found to possess Atlantic salmon on the seas will be presumed *prima facie* to have caught the fish illegally.

Commercial fisheries have depleted food-fish populations that for years seemed infinitely available. After hundreds of years of relentless netting and fishing, anglers in Newfoundland and elsewhere were still catching hundreds of thousands of tons of cod every year in the North Atlantic in the early twentieth century. By the end of World War II, catches were rapidly declining, and industrial fishers began to scour out cod schooling grounds with bottom dredging trawlers. By the early 1970s, only two percent of the aboriginal level of cod populations remained in the great North Banks fishing grounds of the Atlantic. Similar decimations have been visited on haddock. Redfish, plaice, and flounder have been wiped out in one fishing ground after another by relentless commercial fisheries that work fishing grounds harder the fewer fish they find, guaranteeing that no adults

© Paula Leming/PhotoEdit

*Commercial fisheries have not only been brutally efficient in harvesting targeted species of food fish, but have also drastically reduced the populations of commercially undesirable fish and wildlife species—including porpoises and many seabirds.*

*Commercial "longliner" fishermen from Japan and other countries have decimated bluefin tuna populations—while their floating line hooks attract and kill commercially useless species.*

will survive to begin the agonizingly slow struggle of species renewal. (The U.S. National Oceanic and Atmospheric Administration is currently lobbying to enforce minimum size rules for commercially harvested cod, redfish and haddock, which now only apply to sport fishermen. Limits have been set on "bycatch" of regulated species—numbers of cod, haddock, redfish and other species caught by commercial fishers while trawling for other nonregulated species such as dogfish, herring, and hake.) As Farley Mowat wrote in *Sea of Slaughter*, "When a prey animal becomes scarce, its predators normally decrease in numbers, too, permitting the prey an opportunity for recovery. Industrial man works in the opposite way."

Commercial fisheries have not only been brutally efficient in harvesting targeted species for the past three to four hundred years, but have also been indiscriminate in netting commercially undesirable species, killing thousands of "useless" fish as well as seabirds and other creatures. The drift-net fisheries around Greenland trapped hundreds of thousands of seabirds in their nets during the 1960s. Commercial devastation of capelin, silversides, and other baitfish (usually for fertilizer and animal feed) at major Atlantic and Pacific feeding grounds drastically curtailed populations not only of game fish, but also of seals, whales, and seabirds.

It must be remembered, however, that commercial fish-

*Introduction to Saltwater Game Fish · 17*

ermen are not alone in their disregard for the survival of important food and game fish. The slaughter of the great bluefin tuna was engineered in deadly combinations by sport and commercial fishermen, each blinded by greed to the consequences of their actions. In the 1950s, the bluefin was pursued by commercial fishermen who perfected efficient netting methods to catch and kill the fish. Too efficient. After killing 150,000 tons of bluefin in the North Atlantic during the 1950s, commercial netting yielded only two thousand tons by 1973. In 1955, Norwegian netters took ten thousand tons of tuna; in 1973, they managed to find only about one hundred *individual* fish. Portuguese fishermen accustomed to catching thousands of tons of tuna in the fifties and sixties caught only *two* fish in 1972. The Japanese fed a rapacious restaurant and sushi market by using high-tech tuna harvesting that employed purse seiners and long-liners to catch hundreds of thousands of tons of tuna annually during the 1960s. But they paid a steep price: according to Farley Mowat, "By 1980 the entire Japanese fleet of three hundred long-liners only managed to catch four thousand tons of bluefin tuna."

As commercial tuna fishing depleted smaller bluefin populations to the point of unprofitability, sport fishermen waded in to maintain intense pressure on the older, larger, reproducing tuna. The sport-fishing boom for bluefin exploded in the early sixties as thousands of charter boats combed tuna grounds off Long Island and Prince Edward Island during the summer, and Bimini and the Bahamas during the winter. In 1966 alone, 388 giant bluefin were killed off the shores of Newfoundland. As the sushi market boomed in America and Europe, providing charter-boat captains with a lucrative market for landed trophies, they fished the tuna even harder. In 1978, Newfoundland sport fishers caught and sold about three thousand giant tuna to Japan; by 1981, they were able to catch only fifty-five.

Concentrations of bluefin have been found off Prince Edward Island and the Gulf of Saint Lawrence in recent years, although the Newfoundland bluefin have virtually disappeared; however, the numbers of these new schools are in decline from the unharvested tuna school levels of the forties and fifties. It is possible that tuna schools already existed undiscovered in other North Atlantic waters because fishing was concentrated on the "prime" Newfoundland schools. Removing thousands of breeding-age adults from a fish population will reduce numbers of future generations since the pool of spawning adults is drastically smaller: Mothers will not produce more eggs; nature will not allow more fry to survive.

Overfishing can push a species to precariously low numbers. In the late nineteenth and early twentieth centuries, rapacious sport fishing began to eradicate the Atlantic salmon from dozens of prime Canadian spawning waterways: Fishing clubs crowded every major salmon river in Canada, and catches were limitless. Dead salmon were piled up to feed bears and to be distributed to farmers as fertilizer. As World War II passed, commercial fishing, DDT poisoning, and lately, acid rain stepped in to finish the job. The salmon verged on extinction in the most fecund Canadian rivers.

Numbers of captured Miramichi grilse salmon had declined in one survey of Millbank, New Brunswick fishing from two, three, and four thousand per season in the mid-seventies to less than a thousand in 1983. Numbers of multiyear salmon—the twenty and thirty pounders—had declined to less than five hundred catches a season from numbers near two thousand in the seventies, according to a report in *Trout* Magazine in 1987. Aggressive catch and release regulations (only hooked grilse may be kept), and stiff fines against Canadian netters have begun to protect Miramichi salmon runs. But without the cooperation of the angler, the world's noblest game fish might have died out in its favorite river. The same buyout of licenses that benefited Canadian waters generally has also improved the situation on the Miramichi.

Despite this disastrous husbandry of fishery resources, the prospects of some important species have improved, including those of the Atlantic salmon. Although many voices have cried doom over the years, with some justification, many fish species can bounce back from near extinction if given the slimmest margin of safety. In 1906, Jordan and Evermann wrote in *American Food and Game Fishes*:

The trout are rapidly disappearing from trout streams through the agency of the lumberman, manufacturer, and summer boarder. In the words of the late Reverend Myron W. Reed, a noble man, and an excellent angler, "This is the last generation

**The small family commercial fishing boat poses little danger to ocean fish populations.**

of troutfishers. The children will not be able to find any. Already there are well-trodden paths by every stream in Maine, New York, and in Michigan. I know of but one river in North America by the side of which you will find no paper collar or other evidence of civilization. It is the Nameless River. Not that trout will cease to be. They will be hatched by machinery and raised in ponds, and fattened on chopped liver, and grow flabby and lose their spots . . . . The trout that the children will know only by legend is the gold-sprinkled living arrow of the white water; able to zig-zag up the cataract; able to loiter in the rapids; whose dainty meat is the glancing butterfly.

Well, the brook trout *has* disappeared from much of its original habitat, but this apocalyptic scenario has hardly come to pass.

Still, the sporting angler must at least do this to help the conservation of game fish species: Release the fish that will not be eaten. Photographs of the fish can be taken while they are in the water or the net or carefully held in the hand. History teaches an indelible, unavoidable, and tragic lesson: There are only so many fish in the sea.

*Skates, sharks, and rays are cartilaginous as opposed to bony vertebrates.*

# Fundamentals of Saltwater Fish

Ichthyologists classify all fish in two huge groups based on a fundamental anatomical distinction. The *cartilaginous* fish evolved skeletons made only of cartilage; these species are largely found in salt water and are limited to sharks, skates, and rays. In most cartilaginous species, the eggs of the female are fertilized and hatched within her body and the young are born alive. The skates, however, drop their eggs in the sea within a tough, sealed pouch. Cartilaginous fish must sink or swim because they lack the air bladder that allows the *bony* fish to regulate the depth at which they swim. The pelvic fins of a cartilaginous fish have claspers, which facilitate internal fertilization.

Most fish are *bony*—that is, their skeletons are made of bone—and are distinguished from the cartilaginous fish by certain behaviors. The bony fish hatch their young outside the body, in eggs that are expelled and fertilized in nests or *redds*, or simply dropped into open water or over sandy or rocky bottoms. All bony fish have air bladders. The respiratory systems of bony and cartilaginous fish are quite similar, except that most bony fish evolved gill plates rather than the gill slits of sharks and rays. The cetaceans are a distinct class of bony and cartilaginous fish. These mammals of the sea include whales and dolphins. Like other mammals, they have some hair on their bodies at various stages during their life span, are warm-blooded (maintain constant body temperature), and bear their young alive.

*Euryhaline* saltwater fish can tolerate varying levels of salinity, which means they will migrate quite far up estuaries, coastal rivers, and other inshore waters. Tarpon, snook, and ladyfish are some well-known citizens of the euryhaline persuasion.

## Getting the Anatomical News

Most fish in the sea are of the bony variety, as explained above. Except for lampreys, they have two jaws, upper and lower. Fish absorb oxygen from water; they take it in through the mouth, where it passes over the gills in the gill chambers and then passes out through the gill openings. In lampreys, hagfish, sharks, skates, and rays, the gills are covered with skin that passes water in and out through pores or slits; in bony fish, the gills are covered with flaps called opercles. As the gills draw oxygen from the water, it is pumped through the heart and the fish's body. The "used" blood is returned to the heart, where the ventricle expels it to the gills, which release the carbon dioxide into the water. While we lucky land creatures can draw in all the oxygen we need simply by breathing in the air—which is, except in certain highly polluted areas, rich in oxygen—fish must force oxygen-poor water through the gills to draw sufficient oxygen for life. Where water is moving well, they do not have to make any special effort; but in still or poorly oxygenated waters (areas of heavy algae or seaweed, iced-over lakes or ponds), fish must swim to force sufficient water over their gills. Sharks, lacking the swim bladders that allow bony fish to regulate their depth even while stationary, must stay in constant motion to force water over their gills.

Fish propel and guide themselves with their fins, which are membranous and spined in bony fish, and fleshy in cartilaginous fish. The pectoral and pelvic fins grow in pairs. Pectoral fins are located behind the gill covers, in the chest, or behind the head. Ventral and pelvic fins are located on the bottom of the fish, between the throat and the anal fin. The median fins are single and include the dorsal fin, which is found on the back about midway down the fish's body; the caudal fin, which most of us think of as the fish's tail; and the anal fin, which acts as the fish's "rudder," growing on the bottom of the fish just forward of the caudal fin or tail. The number of spines in a particular fin offers a reliable method of identification for many species.

Most predatory fish possess strong eyesight, and ichthyologists for the most part agree that bass, pike, trout, marlin, bluefish, striped bass, tuna, and other freshwater and saltwater fish can discern color. Many fish can see ultraviolet colors invisible to the human eye. At the Woods Hole Marine Biological Laboratory in Massachusetts, researchers discovered that the Japanese dace (*Tribolodon hakonensis*) can see very shortwave ultraviolet color invisible to human beings. A scan of color at this end of the spectrum revealed that every fish bears two stripes on its belly that may help other dace recognize it. Fish communicate through color patterns. When a bluefish female is ready to mate, a bright inflamed spot emerges behind her pectoral fin, the sight of which inflames the ardor of male blues.

Sound travels five times faster in water than in air, and all fish are equipped with a number of sound and vibration detection devices. Nothing demonstrates the extraordinary sensory powers of fish, and their simultaneous need of those powers to survive, than the lateral line. The lateral line is a thin horizontal stripe of open pores running along the side of the fish that act as a combination sense encompassing hearing, touch, and an indefinable radar. It provides what has been called "a sense of distant touch." The pores are extremely sensitive receptors that detect the slightest vibrations in the surrounding water, whether generated by the movement of other fish, noise, or waves. Fish can therefore respond to movements toward or away from them in any direction, including their blind spots in the rear and under the nose. Ichthyologists speculate that the lateral line allows schooling fish to orient themselves in position to one another, thereby creating the most efficient movement possible through the water for each fish. The lateral line also

probably makes it possible for fish to move, attack, and hide at night as well as they do.

The air bladder, present in all bony fish, not only regulates swimming depth but also acts as a detector of sound pressure and waves—at higher frequencies and farther distances (though it does not sense the direction from which the waves are generated) than the lateral line, complementing it to form a complete "radar" detector system. Fish possess an inner ear, which is remarkably similar to that of mammals and other vertebrates, composed of three semicircular canals that serve the equilibrium sense and the otolith organs. In other words, the inner ear helps fish keep their

*Ichthyologists speculate that the lateral line allows schooling fish to orient themselves in position to one another, thereby allowing each fish to move efficiently through the water.*

balance and swim right-side up in water where no light or other stimuli provide visual cues.

The powers of piscine smell are extraordinary. Salmon can detect one part per billion of odorous material in water. They will not use fish ladders (structures designed to give salmon passage over dams and other obstructions) placed in running water in which human hands or bear paws were washed. Salmon kept in swimming pools in which *one drop* of bear-scented water was released exhibited panic activity. Salmon, steelhead, and other anadromous fish (saltwater fish that spawn in freshwater) home in on the freshwater rivers of their birth largely through their sense of smell.

Many saltwater species demonstrate long-distance migration behavior, depending on a combination of sensory information to find their way. Tagged bluefin tuna have traveled from as far as Cat Cay, Bahamas, to Bergen, Norway, a distance of over twenty five hundred miles, in just fifty days. A striped marlin made it from Baja California to Hawaii, about 1,750 miles, at a minimum average speed of forty miles per hour. Changing positions of moon and sun are important navigational cues, as are tidal shifts, sound patterns, visual landmarks, direction of wave fronts in the open sea, and other factors. A.J. McClane explains in *Game Fish of North America* the importance of magnetic sensitiv-

© Tim Choate

**The sailfish has highly developed predatory instincts, and will work with other adult sails to herd baitfish into tight groups or "balls" so they can be easily attacked.**

ity in long-distance migration: "The earth's geomagnetic field can provide direction, time and location of local landmarks, and laboratory work in Hawaii has already demonstrated that tropical tuna have enough of a highly magnetic iron oxide in their ethmoid sinuses to respond to magnetic conditioning experiments."

Bottom feeders such as the drum, flounder, wrasse, and sturgeon rely almost exclusively on their sense of smell to uncover the vegetative jetsam, shellfish, grasses, and goodies they enjoy buried in sandy bottoms or under rocks, reefs, and other structures. Black bass, tarpon, and other night predators need a keen sense of smell to find elusive baitfish. Baitfish possess an acute sense of smell that helps them avoid predators. It was found that minnows in an enclosed tank could distinguish the odors of fifteen different related fish species, and exhibited alarm when the odorous chemical emitted by the injured skin of their species was released in the water.

Clearly, fish are evolutionary marvels at hunting, finding, and attacking prey. This is good news for the angler: Those fishermen who can present lures and baits in ways that best appeal to the predatory senses of their quarry are bound to enjoy great success.

# All In The Family

Whenever and wherever marlin and tuna are being caught consistently, world records are a possibility; it is therefore important to identify precisely what species of fish are brought on board. The following family trees not only provide an overview of the relationships within two major game fish tribes, but outline key identification information for the pelagic game-fish angler.

# ISTIOPHORIDAE OF NORTH AMERICA

Prolonged, rounded upper jaw or bill, body is dark above and pale below, narrow-lobed caudal fin
with 2 horizontal keels, 2 dorsal fins and 2 anal fins.

---

### Makaira nigricans
(Blue marlin)
Height of front dorsal lobe fin does not exceed body depth; lateral line branches into net of hexagons

### Makaira indica
(Black marlin)
Can be identified by the rigid pectoral fin that cannot be folded flat against the body without breaking the joints, barely visible lateral line that is a straight double row of pores. The first dorsal fin is proportionately the lowest of any billfish, less than 50 percent of body depth

### Tetrapturus audax
(Striped marlin)
Easily identified by its high, pointed first dorsal fin, equaling or exceeding its greatest body depth; pointed anal and pectoral fins; straight, single and clearly visible lateral line

### Istiophorus platypterus
(Sailfish)
Height of front dorsal lobe exceeds body depth; near part of first dorsal fin sail-like, single canal lateral line; first dorsal and first anal fin spotted

### Tetrapterus plfuegeri
(Longbill spearfish)
Height of front dorsal fin lobe exceeds body depth; single canal lateral line; first dorsal and first anal fins unspotted

# SCOMBRIDAE OF NORTH AMERICA

### (Tuna and mackerel)

Finlets behind dorsal and anal fins, deep notch between first and second dorsal fins, very slender caudal peduncle. Tuna can maintain body temperatures noticeably higher than that of surrounding waters.

---

### GENUS AUXIS

Scales on front of body extended only past gill area—this feature is called a corselet. First and second dorsal fins are far apart

### GENUS EUTHYNNUS

(Tuna)

Scales on front of body to corselet, first and second dorsal fin spines set close together

---

### Auxis thazard

(Frigate mackerel)
1–5 spots below pectoral fin; unscaled back has 15 or more narrow, oblique dark lines

### Auxis rochei

(Bullet mackerel)
No spots below pectoral fin; dark, nearly vertical bars on unscaled back

### Euthynnus alletteratus

(Little tunny)
4–5 dark spots below pectoral fin, no dark stripes on belly, dorsal fins connected at base, short pectoral fin

### Euthynnus affinis

(Kawakawa: Indo-Pacific)
Scaleless except for corselet and lateral line; at midpoint of dorsal fin a pattern of squiggly, oblique lines spreads over back from lateral line to tail; 14–16 dorsal fin spines; short pectoral fin

### Thunnus alalunga

(Albacore)
Very long pectoral fin, wedge-shaped body, dorsal finlets yellow, near edge of caudal fins white

### Euthynnus pelamis

(Skipjack tuna)
Dorsal fins connected at base, short pectoral fin, 3–5 black stripes on belly, 14–18 spines in first dorsal fin

### Thunnus albacares

(Yellowfin tuna)
Moderately long pectoral fin, second dorsal fin and all finlets yellow, no white near edge of caudal fin, golden-yellow stripe on flank

### Thunnus obesus

(Bigeye tuna)
Moderately long pectoral fins, pointed head, dusky dorsal and anal fins, 12–14 spines on first dorsal fin, bright yellow finlets

## GENUS SARDA

## GENUS SCOMBER
First and second dorsal fins widely separated

## GENUS SCOMBEROMORUS
At least 15–16 dorsal fin spines

### Acanthocybium solanderi
(Wahoo)
Elongate jaws form a beak, long, low first dorsal fin

### Sarda sarda
(Atlantic bonito)
Entire body scaled, 7 or more oblique dark stripes on back, 20–22 dorsal fin spines, distinctly wavy lateral line, scaled body with distinct corselet of scales around gills

### Sarda chiliensis
(Pacific bonito)
Gulf of Alaska to Chile, slanted lines on back, entire body scaled

### Scomber japonicus
(Chub mackerel)
30 wavy black bars across body to just below lateral line, silvery below with dusky blotches, lacks corselet of scales seen on many mackerel, entire body scaled

### Scomber scombrous
(Atlantic mackerel)
Back crossed by 20–23 broad black vertical wavy bars, no spots below lateral line, lacks corselet of scales

### Scomberomorus cavalla
(King mackerel)
Lateral line drops precipitously below second dorsal fin, 15–16 dorsal fin spines, 8–9 gill rakers

### Scomberomorus regalis
(Cero)
Lateral line slops evenly downward, first dorsal fin black, 17–18 dorsal fin spines, 15–18 gill rakers

### Scomberomorus maculatus
(Spanish mackerel)
First dorsal fin black, 17–18 dorsal fin spines, 13–15 gill rakers

Grouper in a coral reef hold where, protected and camouflaged, he is difficult, if not impossible, to attack.

# Getting Them Where They Live

Studying undersea habitats is vitally important to the angler or wildlife enthusiast who wants to understand the links between how fish behave and where they prefer to live. North Atlantic open seas, Caribbean deep blue waters, tropical reefs, shallow tidal flats, deep sea wrecks, Pacific estuaries, saltwater marshes, Florida mangrove rivers, Central American flats, New England surf: Each of these habitats provides the best combination of shelter, food supply, light, and water temperature for particular species. Saltwater fishing more often than not involves fishing a particular sort of water, or habitat, for a range of related species rather than one particular fish. The blue-water charter boater rigs his or her skip baits to catch any number of fast-swimming pelagic species. The reef fisher is "grab-bagging" for all sorts of fish. The giant bottom-fishing party boats will haul up flatfish, tautog, cod, and many other species. The flats fisher is often equipped to catch tarpon *or* bonefish *or* permit. The surf fisher, who baits his or her own hook, and makes individual decisions about where and how to fish will be prepared to pursue any number of species, depending on which fish are running or biting.

Here are the major oceanic habitats, with the leading game fish one can reasonably expect to encounter in them. But oceanic fish do move around a great deal, and will often be found where one least expects them: This list provides only their most likely hangouts.

*Flounder live on the sea bottom, and different species develop appropriate matching coloration to disguise their presence on the ocean floor.*

## SHALLOW TIDAL WATERS OVER SAND AND VEGETATION, FLATS

*Warm Water*
tarpon, permit, ladyfish, bonefish, machete, horse-eye jack, spotted sea trout, barracuda, jack crevalle

*Cold and Temperate Water*
weakfish, striped bass

## ESTUARIES, BRACKISH COASTAL RIVERS, AND INLETS

*Warm Water*
snook, tarpon, jack crevalle, spotted sea trout, Atlantic croaker, red drum, black drum, gulf flounder, cubera snapper

*Cold and Temperate Water*
white sea bass, Atlantic tomcod, striped bass, weakfish

## DEEP, SMOOTH SEA BOTTOMS

*Warm Water*
gulf flounder, diamond turbot, naked sole

*Warm and Temperate Water*
Pacific tomcod, Pacific ocean whitefish, African pompano, jack crevalle, Pacific halibut, California halibut, English sole

*Cold Water*
cod, haddock, hake, rock sole, winter flounder, lingcod, Atlantic halibut

## OFFSHORE SHELVES AND CHANNELS DROP-OFFS

*Warm Water*
yellowtail, permit, palometa, bigeye trevally, southern kingfish, Atlantic croaker, red drum

*Cold and Temperate Water*
striped bass, bluefish, white sea bass, weakfish, redtail surfperch, black perch, rainbow seaperch, corbina

## SHALLOW REEFS, SHALLOW ROCKY BOTTOMS, KELP BEDS, AND ISLAND CHANNELS

*Warm and Temperate Water*
black grouper, jack crevalle, horse-eye jack, yellowtail, red snapper, yellowtail snapper, barracuda, bigeye trevally, cubera snapper

*Cold and Temperate Water*
jack mackerel, redtail surfperch, black perch, kelp perch, striped seaperch, walleye seaperch, tautog

## OPEN OFFSHORE OCEAN SURFACE AND MIDDLE DEPTHS

*Warm Water*
cobia, rainbow runner, cerra, amberjack, wahoo, dolphin, skipjack tuna, chub mackerel, king mackerel, bigeye tuna, sailfish, spearfish, redfish

*Warm and Temperate Water*
bluefish, Atlantic bonito, bullet mackerel, little tunny, Spanish mackerel, albacore, yellowfin tuna, bluefin tuna, swordfish, blue and black marlin, white marlin, sailfish, striped marlin

*Cold Water*
Atlantic mackerel, Atlantic salmon

## TIDAL AND SURF ZONES AROUND STRUCTURES—PILES, PIERS, BRIDGES, JETTIES

*Cold, Temperate, or Warm Water*
Pacific tomcod, Atlantic tomcod, sheepshead, walleye surfperch, striped seaperch, rainbow seaperch

## DEEP ROCKY BOTTOMS; DEEP REEFS, WRECKS

*Warm Water*
black sea bass, red grouper, Nassau grouper, kelp bass, red snapper, yellowtail snapper

**Warm and Temperate Water**
giant sea bass, African pompano, boccacio, rockfish

*Cold Water*
*pollock, tautog*

**Baitfish populations near coral reefs provide forage for vast numbers of smaller predators such as snapper and yellowtail that, in turn, are the prey of barracuda and other dominant species.**

# The Angler's Arsenal

It is as true today as it has been for thousands of years: You will know a good fisher by his or her *successful* fish-catching idiosyncrasies. However, before you can create, you must know the fundamentals: This is as true of fishing rigs as it is of poetry. *Saltwater Game Fish of North America* will cover the time-honored methods for catching each fish cataloged, as well as a few innovative techniques gaining popularity with fishing pros and angling writers.

Generally, tackle does more of the work in hooking the fish for the saltwater angler than it does for the freshwater angler; trolling is by far the most productive saltwater angling method, which means the boat does most of the work—until the fish is hooked. Then the angler had better be using strong, well-maintained tackle that can handle long runs, headshaking jumps, the abrasion of rocks and other structures, and sharp, cutting teeth, gill covers, and tails. Thus, saltwater terminal tackle is usually more complicated than that used in freshwater. Big-game fishing requires sophisticated trolling tackle linked with swivels, various leaders, snaps, spinners, flashers, attractors, snells, hooks, and strong monofilament or braided fishing line. Surf and flats fishing are less complicated, but the self-sufficient angler must know a range of terminal tackle setups, including swivel, sinker, and hook rigs, as well as effective lures and baits.

The lure or bait is the most important element of an angler's tackle, for if the game fish does not strike the angler's offering nothing else will matter. Good anglers know what bait, fish, or lure game fish will probably hit, and smart fishermen bring plenty of supplies. Know all the fish-catching tools available: The more you use, the more fish you will catch. The following list defines the important lure types used by the successful saltwater angler:

*This little tunny—a fine light tackle sportfish—grabbed a rubber squid trolling lure.*

© Chris Huss

**The blue shark has become one of the most popular sport fish on the Atlantic seaboard, largely because they are very easy to catch once found—indeed, anglers often catch the same shark they released earlier in the day.**

# Lures

## Swimming Plugs

A plug is any lure shaped to imitate a swimming or struggling fish that, when retrieved, "swims" on top or beneath the water. Plugs are usually designed to suggest a wounded or struggling creature that would make easy prey for the feeding game fish. Swimming plugs run beneath the surface, either at shallow or middle depths; they can be cast or trolled. Leading manufacturers of the best saltwater plugs include Cotton Cordell, Roberts, Stan Gibbs, Rebel, Rapala, Boone, Creek Chub, Arbogast, Luhr-Jensen, and Cisco Kid.

## Floating Divers

These specialized plugs rest on the surface after the cast and then dive under water and swim beneath the surface during retrieve with a wobbling eat-me-I'm-helpless action. Different floating divers are designed to swim at various levels under water. Largely used by surf casters, these torpedo-shaped plugs should be fished with slow, intermittent jerks of the rod. Technically, no trolling lure could be called a floating diver since the static floating of a lure plays no role in catching fish from a moving boat. Cordell Red Fins and Arbogast Hammerheads are held in high esteem by many surf fishers.

## Poppers

The popper is a surface-disturbing plug. It attracts predatory interest by gurgling, bubbling, and popping on the water surface as it buries its wide open mouth in the chop during the surf angler's vigorous retrieves. Indeed, the popper can be sensibly used only in surf-casting situations, where larger predators are feeding near the surface and the angler has the leverage to really work the big plug through the surface water. Stan Gibbs and Creek Chub make some of the best surf-casting poppers available.

© Allan Weitz

*Smaller gamefish such as this bonito can be pursued with large plugs and bait casting tackle, allowing the angler the thrill of casting to sighted fish.*

## Diamond Jigs

This simple lure looks like a long, narrow, four-sided spoon and is fished like a jig. The traditional diamond jig is made of plain reflective steel, cut long with four sides, and tapered at the top and bottom. Newer lures that fall into this category are shaped like eels or finished with scales, Mylar™ strips, and other features. Bridgeport, Ava, Newell, and Glen Evans are the top manufacturers.

© Tim Choate

*This magnificent marlin grabbed a trolling lure, attracted by its skipping and skimming motion along the surface of the sea on the arms of the outrigger.*

## Knife-Handle Jigs

These lures, pounded flatter and shorter than diamond jigs, are usually finished with scalelike indents or nicks. Generally made of steel or brass, and chrome-plated or painted, the knife-handle jig does look like a knife handle, and it is often rigged with a tuft of bucktail, or feather, or soft plastic tail. These popular surf-casting lures are retrieved through the surf where their wobbling, flashing actions draw more than their share of bluefish, weakfish, and striper strikes. The knife-handle, diamond, and tin-lure jigs can all be tipped with a piece of pork rind to help predators find the lure with their noses as well as their eyes. Hopkins, Bridgeport, and Kastmaster are the standard names among knife-handle-jig makers; the No=Eql and Shorty jigs can be found in just about any surf caster's tackle box.

## Trolling Lures

These soft plastic and rubber items are designed for top-water trolling at various speeds. Trolling lures attract fish by skipping and skimming on the water surface when out-rigged behind the boat. Different trolling lures are designed to work best in particular ranges of speed, depending on the design of the lure head. Squarish lure heads are designed for slower trolling; more streamlined, bullet-shaped heads work properly at faster clips. Jet lures are the high-rpm models that will skip and swim like the fastest flying fish at speeds of up to seventeen knots. Johnson's Mold Craft, Sevenstrand, Tony Acetta, and Illander are among the long-standing makers of reliable products. Popular models include the Konahead, Sevenstrand Clone, Tony Acetta Jelly Belly, and Mold Craft Swimmer.

## Eel Skin Rigs

Perhaps no lure catches more fish in the surf than an eel skin rig, of which stripers are especially fond. The core of the lure is a lead head jig built with a stiff, thin wire onto which the angler fits a real eel skin. The rig is fished with slow twitches of the rod tip, which impart a swimming motion irresistible to predators.

## Weighted Bucktails

This is a lead-headed jig dressed with a variety of materials, including natural bucktail, synthetic hair, feathers, plastic, or rubber strips. The bucktail can be jigged off piers and docks or surf cast (the angler "hops" the lure on and off the bottom to attract bottom-cruising crushers like the striped bass or drum).

## Plastic Squids

These lures are extremely effective on a wide range of species. Their name tells you just what they are: soft plastic or rubber molded to look like squid of various sizes. Because so many game fish love the real thing, these lures might be the highest-percentage method available to the saltwater fisher. Various models can be trolled, jigged, cast, or slowly deep-trolled for tuna, marlin, dolphin, sailfish, amberjack, bluefish, striper, black bass, chinook and coho salmon, tarpon, and many other top game fish. Leading manufacturers include Moldcraft, Sevenstrand, and Applied Oceanographic.

## Tin Squids

These rectangular flattish spoons are made from block tin, a burnished, soft, translucent metal that some traditional surf casters claim is far more effective at catching fish in moving surf than the common bright reflective finishes seen on most steel lures. Once the staple of surf fishermen, the tin squid has fallen in popularity as more and more plug and jig models have arrived on today's tackle market.

# Bottom Fishing

## Using Float and Sinker Rigs

Let's face it: When you fish on the ocean, you can't afford to get skunked. The fly fisherman or bass caster can walk down to the local stream and toss a couple of casts for an hour and go home without a fish, ennobled by the contact with nature. However, a saltwater fishing expedition usually requires an investment of time and money sufficient to create the angler's desire for a substantial return. Many anglers rely on the highest-percentage fishing method of all—live bait—to get results. There's no arguing that using the actual creatures and foods preferred by the predators will bring the best results, largely because live bait calls on all of the predator's attack senses: sight, smell, and lateral line. Below is a menu of basic rigs for presenting live bait to game fish with a variety of feeding habits.

## Sinker Rigs

### The Basic Bottom Rig

Attach a three-way swivel to the line; add a bank sinker and snelled hook to each eye. Use from boats for bottom bouncing and drifting, or still fishing from docks and piers.

### Spreader Rig

Spreader rigs make it possible to fish two, three, or even four baits at once from the same rod and reel without tangling or crossing lines. Is it great sport? No. Does it catch many fish? Yes. The fishing line is tied to a spreader, which is a swivel with jutting wire arms that end in round eyes. Join snelled hooks to the round eyes. A crosslock or Pompanette snap joins a dropsy sinker to the bottom of the spreader swivel. *Bon appetit!*

## Sliding Sinker Rig

A flexible bottom rig for all kinds of deep water bait fishing. The line is linked to the swivel with a snelled hook below. An egg sinker is strung above the swivel, which slides up and down the fishing line, so that the fish won't feel the weight when it takes the bait.

## Fluke Rig

The fishing line is joined to a leader with a three-way swivel from which a dropsy, or bank sinker, is tied to sink the rig. A spinning flasher is mounted above the hook to attract the attention of lethargic, weird-looking flounder. Use as many spinners or flashers as desired.

*Multiple-hook rigs allow sport and commercial anglers to catch maximum numbers of "keepers" over a limited period of time.*

## Breakaway Rig

When fishing rough bottoms, wrecks, reefs, or other heavily obstructed environments, anglers tie the sinker to break off when it gets snagged so the entire rig is not lost. Connect the fishing line to a hook with a swivel, and then tie the sinker to the swivel, with an extremely light piece of monofilament.

## Deep Trolling Rig

In this rig, the bait or lure is trolled as deep as need be, but the leader and fishing line are jointed by a three-way swivel from which a dropsy sinker is trailed to keep the lure or bait off the bottom.

## Bottom Trolling Rig

For those game fish working the lower depths. From the bottom up, rig it this way: A jig, feather, or spoon will be trolled behind a three- to twenty-five-foot leader of mono or wire, depending on the dental work of the prey. The leader links to a bead-chain swivel (to facilitate line rotation), which links to a torpedo or keel sinker attached to another bead-chain swivel joined to the main line. Depending on the trolling depth required, lead core or wire lines may be necessary.

## Fishfinder Rig

Favored by surf casters, this setup frees the action of the hook and line from the sinker, which is attached to the line above the swivel with a connecting link snap. Pyramid sinkers are preferred for their anchoring ability in soft sand. The bait floats free in the water, often buoyed off the bottom with a float or cork attached to the swivel. Fish can dine on your bait with no "sinker sense"—which means that you will eventually dine on them.

# Float Rigs

## Bottom Rig Float

A float can keep the bait suspended above the very bottom, where crabs and less desirable fish can nibble it off. A small barrel float can be attached between a spreader rig or single hook and the main line. Try tying the sinker on the bottom of the rig, adding a float above a short length of line, then above the float, tying the swivel, spreader, and hooks (often called an Angling Jenny after the trademark rig made by the Oberlin Canteen Company).

## Drifting Flounder Rig

This rig allows anglers to jig baits in moving tides and currents while maintaining uniform depth. A large quill sliding float is attached above a sinker or swivel at the desired depth of line below the swivel to allow free movement of the bait. A sinker is attached to a three-way swivel, which also connects to the snelled hook and bait.

## Simple Bottom Float Rig

Not too effective when tides or currents are strong, but perfect for fishing bait with a "light touch" to wary middle- and bottom-zones feeders in *shallow* waters, this rig is a variation of the floating globe-and-worm setup used on ponds by children. Tie on a barrel or tube float above the correct amount of line for the depth you want to reach, rig your hook with bait, and cast. When the float dips under the surface, give it a yank.

## Float Popper Rig

This is similar to the previous rig, but a hollow-face popping float may be used, allowing the angler to pop the float with the rod tip, attracting fish to the bait.

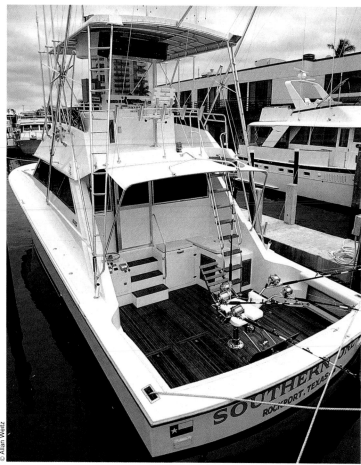

© Allan Weitz

**Short fiberglass rods, outriggers, and heavy-duty trolling reels are the necessary tools for big-game fishing.**

# A Note on Boat Tackle

In discussing fishing techniques through this book, I will often recommend *boat tackle* as appropriate for anglers going after the larger pelagic game fish. This is the generic name for trolling tackle approved by the IGFA (International Game Fish Association). That includes rods, reels, and line. These big-game rods and lines are usually divided into certified weight classes: 13-lb., 18-lb., 22-lb., 33-lb., 53-lb., and so on up to 132-lb. tackle. The test refers to the strength of the line, and each class of line can be matched to a rod of the right length, flexibility, and weight. Most trolling rods are thick sticks of no more than seven feet and no less than six feet in overall length; they are fixed with at least five roller guides to cool down wire line friction and resist abrasion.

Super-tough tubular fiberglass is the construction material of choice.

Trolling reels are classified by the O (for ocean) system, with the lightest reel starting at 2/0 and the heaviest designated as 12/0. The reel numbers roughly correspond to pound test, with 2/0 reels generally suited to 20-lb. test, 3/0 reels to 30-lb. test, and so forth up to 12/0. Trolling reels, usually cut from solid bar aluminum, are fitted with precision-engineered drag systems. The drag function is crucial in fighting pelagic game, both in controlling the first post-strike run of the hooked fish and tiring it through the middle and final stages of the battle. Larger reels are fitted with harness lugs on the end plate, which allow the angler in the fighting chair to secure his or her reel to the shoulder or kidney harness. (Fighting chairs, which allow the angler to use leg and back power in resisting the mighty run of the enemy, are crucial to successful big-game fishing.)

Over the years and through the consensus of North American anglers, the fish selected for discussion here have earned the title of game fish. Anglers in the course of pursuing particular species will catch a huge variety of fish, and grab-bag fishing for any species that will take bait on a reef bottom or around a sunken wreck offers a good deal of interest and action to casual sport fishers, but most anglers, angling writers, and captains reserve the apellation game fish for a select pantheon of species. The criteria have been established through the common experience of anglers, and the river of angling literature that ranges from mimeographed newsletters to classic books. The qualities that game fish share include: an ability to fight vigorously reflecting the strength and energy of a predator; a preference for live fish and other creatures as food; a degree of selectivity in diet influenced by times of the day and year, water conditions, food availability, spawning habits, and other factors; and an inclination to hunt and hide in identifiable and interesting patterns that add the element of gaming to the angler's challenge. It is certainly true that beauty of coloration and balance of proportion in the body of a fish add to its appeal as a game fish, though this is a sufficient, and not a necessary condition of that designation.

The species described here include those saltwater species most sought after by sport fishermen in the waters of North America.

© M. Timothy O'Keefe/Tom Stack & Associates

**Those who would pursue the ocean's largest predators, from swordfish to billfish to tuna, must be very patient.**

Meet the Game Fish

IPA

RT2

# BARRACUDA

*T*he truth is that the barracuda is among the finest game fishes in the world. Of course it's a killer, but so is every other fish that swims; a barracuda is only more efficient.

—Erwin A. Bauer, *The Saltwater Fisherman's Bible*

*GREAT BARRACUDA*

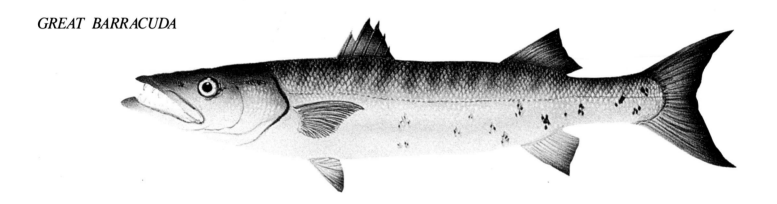

**Range**
The great barracuda, as it is called in Atlantic and Caribbean waters, ranges from northern Florida to Brazil, from the Bahamas to the Virgin Islands. The Pacific or California barracuda is most commonly found from central California south to Mexico's Baja Peninsula.

**Color**
The barracuda has a dark green or bluish-grey back that lightens to bright silver flanks and a white belly marked with greyish black vertical bars and dark splotches from midbody to tail.

**Identifying characteristics**
The long, silvery, slender body and full set of razor-sharp canine teeth make the barracuda an unmistakable fish in the tropical Atlantic or Pacific.

**Size**
The great barracuda of the Atlantic grows much larger than its West Coast cousin. The big choppers of the Keys, the Caribbean, and deeper waters will often tip the scales at forty pounds or more, and anglers can easily catch barracuda between ten and twenty pounds. Juvenile three- to four-pound Atlantic 'cuda are extremely willing game fish that will strike a variety of lures or even flies. The existing IGFA barracuda world record is an 85-pounder taken off Christmas Island (in the East Indian

*'Cuda can't resist brightly-colored tube lures rapidly retrieved.*

© James D. Watt

*Smaller barracuda, particularly the Pacific barracuda, will travel in schools. Larger adults are inveterate loners.*

Ocean) in 1992. Pacific barracuda rarely grow over ten pounds, and most weigh between one and three pounds. Pacific barracuda are a wild, leaping sport fish when caught on light tackle, and as such are an excellent choice for the saltwater fly fisherman.

**Spawning period**

May through June is when the Pacific barracuda spawn. The great barracuda's spawning behavior is triggered by changes in water temperature. When barracuda habitat reaches temperatures of about seventy-three degrees, males and females begin to ripen for spawning. Mating takes place over late spring and all of summer, with many barracuda waiting until September to reproduce. Spawning behavior ceases when October and November bring dropping water temperatures.

**Angling notes**

The barracuda is a vicious predator that feeds with absolutely indiscriminate aggression when young but becomes much more selective after reaching adulthood. Great barracuda frequent tropical Atlantic reefs, tidal channels, island shelves and drop-offs, flats, and even surf waters in their endless patrols for easy meals and no-hassle excitement. The great barracuda is a maverick predator, always on the move.

Pacific barracuda frequent surf zones and reef waters in the southern Pacific. All barracuda are very good at making meals of crippled or wounded fish, and a flashing silver spoon or lure is a magnetic draw for barracuda strikes. Barracuda also love multicolored eel and silvery needlefish lures, which draw more chopper strikes on average than any other artificial lure.

Smaller fish may travel in schools, but larger adults are invariably loners. A medium-weight barracuda hooked on a light saltwater spinning or fly rod will provide very rousing combat. A big chopper on the line will burn off a hundred yards of line, jump, run again, and

© Chris Huss

*Large adult choppers single out wounded or otherwise distressed fish for their meals.*

jump some more before burning out.

Great barracuda, common throughout the Keys and Bahamas, are prime targets for captains and guides from the Gulf coast of Florida to the Lesser Antilles of the Caribbean.

Barracuda in both the Atlantic and Pacific are among those tropical fish species infected with the *ciguatera* virus that makes their flesh poisonous to humans. Though not every fish is ciguatoxic, barracuda should never be eaten.

**Lures** Any silvery spoon or jig will attract a smaller barracuda, and it will often attract the big ones if the lure is retrieved very fast with lots of action. Needlefish and brightly colored tube lures attract hot strikes if given a red-hot retrieve. Anglers should cast lures away from the barracuda and retrieve them at a fast clip just by its nose. Standard blue-silver and silver plugs will see some success, as will the occa-

sional rubber squid or feather. Barracuda are very unpredictable; they will strike at any number of lures or baits depending on their hunger, their mood, and the availability of food. Barracuda don't like to invest too much work or time into hunting food; instead, they love poaching small, injured or otherwise vulnerable baitfish for a quick and easy dinner. Anglers are wise to remember this when fishing artificial lures.

**Bait** Trolled or skipped mullet, live chum, or yellowtails hooked beneath a float are irresistible to 'cuda large and small.

**Flies** Streamer flies such as the Lee Cuddy are effective if brought to the chopper's attention.

**Best tackle** Light to medium saltwater spinning or bait-casting rods of bigger length and slow-taper; 10- to 15-lb.-test line. Barracuda fishing requires a ten- to twelve-inch wire leader.

# STRIPED BASS

*M*en cannot become fish, nor can fish transform themselves into men. But over the centuries, men have learned to appreciate in creatures qualities that are also recognizable in humans. Men who know the striper know it to be a creature of strength and sinew, endowed with unique determination to survive.

—John Cole, *Striper*

*STRIPED BASS*

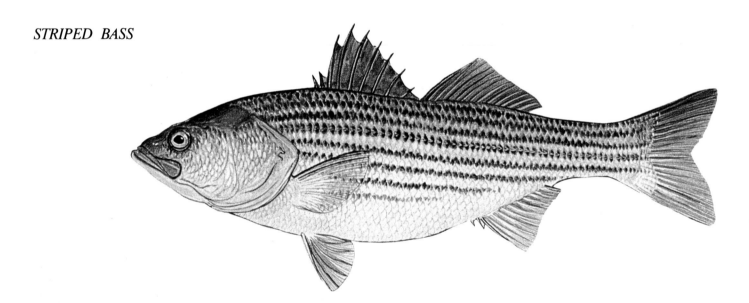

**Range**  Stripers occur the length of the Atlantic coast from northern Florida to the Gulf of Saint Lawrence. Hatchery planting in the nineteenth century opened the Pacific coast to striped bass, where they now live in great numbers from San Diego to the Columbia River. The striped bass have also flourished in coastal freshwater lakes and rivers in southern states, including Louisiana, Mississippi, and South Carolina.

**Color**  The blackish back of the striper brightens to silver flanks and belly, and the body has thin, vertical black stripes.

**Identifying characteristics**  Most old hands know the striper by its double dorsal fins and the horizontal black stripes on its flanks. It has a large mouth with a protruding lower jaw, the posterior edge of the opercle has two flat spines, and the first dorsal fin has eight to ten strong spines.

**Size** Stripers vary greatly in size. The IGFA record is a seventy-eight-pound, three-ounce bass caught in the waters off Atlantic City, New Jersey, in 1982.

**Spawning period** The anadromous striper migrates into fresh or brackish water to spawn between late April and early June in water temperatures of around sixty-five degrees. Striped bass eggs will not

hatch above seventy degrees. The pollution of many of the striper's favorite East Coast spawning areas, including Chesapeake Bay and the Hudson River, has severely limited the survival rate of eggs, larvae, and fry by raising water temperatures, fouling river bottoms, and raising chemical pollutant levels. The fouling of striped bass spawning beds has sparked enormous controversy between development interests and preservationists. A prominent example is the ten-year battle between city developers and ecologists (among other objectors) over the Westway Highway project in New York City, which would

*Anglers have caught fewer striped bass in recent years, as pollution has destroyed favorite striper watersheds and spawning grounds, including the Chesapeake Bay and the Hudson River. Some naturalists and ichthyologists believe the species is finally on the rebound.*

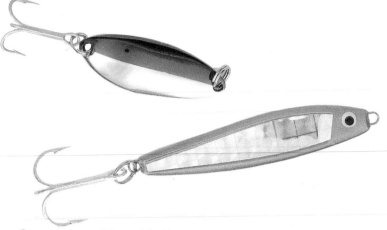

*Spoons, tin squids, and knife-handle jigs are favorite lures for striper surf-fishermen.*

*Exact migratory patterns of East and West Coast stripers are still unknown.*

have destroyed one of the last remaining spawning grounds in the Hudson River for North Atlantic striped bass.

**Angling notes**  Striped bass have declined dramatically over the past twenty years, as pollution has decimated favorite striper watersheds that include the Chesapeake and the Hudson; acid rain has killed young striper larvae and fry; and commercial fishermen have taken far too many spawning-age female stripers. The commercial catch of stripers from Maine to North Carolina dropped from about 14.7 million pounds in 1973 to approximately 1.7 million pounds in 1983. Strict embargoes on commercial and sport fishing have improved the results of striper spawning cycles (as has water improvement in the Hudson and other watersheds). The May 24, 1988 issue of *The New York Times* reported that striped bass populations are rapidly increasing: "Government biologists and conservationists warn that the return of the striped bass is fragile. The future of the fish will not be secure, they insist, unless the water pollution and the acid rain that threaten its habitat and repro-

ductive processes are controlled."

The exact migratory patterns of East and West Coast stripers are still unknown, although icthyologists and angling experts can project where stripers are most likely to congregate during the year. Some striper schools are extremely active, traveling the length of the Atlantic seaboard. Other striper clans, including those found in large schools in Chesapeake Bay, remain in the same watershed for life. Good striper fishermen will chart the migrations of local schools and concentrate their fishing efforts at those times when the bass are running. Anyone interested in pursuing striped bass should talk to tackle-shop pros, other anglers, and their local game wardens about when to fish the best bass runs of the year in their area.

Striped bass can be caught with virtually any saltwater fishing rig, from a surf-casting outfit to a jigging rod and reel used from a pier. These voracious game fish hit a variety of plugs and when hungry, the fish will eat any kind of live (or dead) bait. There's plenty of good striped bass fishing to be found

© Jim P. Garrison

*Stripers have flourished in freshwater habitats. This 15-pound beauty was taken in an Oklahoma impoundment.*

*Dungeness Stinger casting plug—perfect for surf casting.*

around the shores and even lakes of North America, since stocking programs in South Carolina, Arizona, and the West Coast have dug in, caught hold, and produced fine striper populations. The Santee and Cooper lakes in South Carolina are home to a huge striped bass population. Coastal striper hot spots include Montauk, Long Island, Block Island, the north New Jersey shore, Race Point at Provincetown, Cape Cod, Newport, Rhode Island, the San Francisco Bay on the West Coast, and the Umpqua River in Oregon.

In most striped bass hot spots, night fishing is far more profitable because at night the cruising striped bass move close to shore and up tidal rivers on aggressive feeding runs. Prospective surf casters not only need to know when the fish are running, but they also must examine the topography of the beach waters and beyond at low tide. Where are the tide rips, gullies, drop-offs, and holes? Where do slicks in rough water indicate deeper holes that might hide big stripers? Stripers love active, churning water where they can find bait fish suspended in the thrall of the tide. Eelgrass beds and mussel-studded flats are also extremely likely striper hunting grounds. The striped bass also love sand eels with the passion of a New Yorker for Chinese food, and at night they will charge into East Coast tidal waters, surf zones,

estuaries, and brackish rivers to slurp up eels by the hundreds. In rivers and surf zones where the eels are plentiful, surf casters and fly fisherman can experience some of the best night fishing available on the East Coast of the United States.

The most efficient, if least sexy, method of taking stripers is deep wireline trolling, especially off Long Island and New Jersey where stripers run in the deep oceanic banks known to cap-

*Light baitcasting tackle is perfectly adequate for smaller freshwater stripers.*

tains in these waters. The largest fish off Montauk Point and Block Island are often taken with live eel drift-fishing in the banks and off buoys and light-houses.

**Lures**    Although difficult, surf casting is probably the most popular form of striped bass fishing on the Atlantic seaboard. The Reverse Atom, Danny, Goo-Goo Eyes, Stan Gibbs Polaris and Darter, Cotton Cordell Red Fin, Striper Swiper, Arbogast Mud Bug, Chopper Popper, Salty Boogie, and other popping plugs and jointed lures are favored by many surf casters, and are especially effective when fished noisily on the surface at night. Tin squids and large

knife-handle jigs, including the Hopkins Shorty or No=Eql, often succeed when the stripers are in the surf. The rigged eel or eel skin probably catches more striped bass than any other rig, and it is made by fitting an eel skin on a large lead-head jig and retrieving it with an undulating motion.

**Bait**    Sandworms, bloodworms, soft-shell crabs, menhaden, and squid are all tempting bait for the always-hungry striped bass. These can be surf cast or suspended off the bottom with a float rig on heavy nylon or wire leaders and 20- to 30-lb.-test line.

**Best tackle**    For surf casting, ten- to twelve-foot fast-taper (the rod's tip is "whippy" and soft for slinging long casts) surf-casting rods and heavy spinning reels are best; jigging and boat casting require shorter, sturdier rods. Bottom trolling with live bait requires a short glass jigging or medium-weight trolling or bait-casting rod fitted with 20- to 30-lb.-test swiveled to a six-foot leader snelled to a size 5/0 or 7/0 hook and the bait.

Anglers are urged to check with their state Fish and Game Commission or provincial authority for size and limit regulations. The striper is still fighting off extinction on the East Coast (no one knows how their eggs and new young will fare each spring in the face of pollution). Whatever the local regulations, handle captured fish with care, know the state or provincial recommendations on eating stripers from polluted waters, and, unless you're absolutely committed to eating the fish, send it back to the ocean where the struggle to propagate and survive may continue.

© Jim P. Garrison

*Striper fishing on Lake Texahoma, Oklahoma.*

# BLUEFISH

## (Snapper, Tailor, Marine Piranha)

When all is said and done, I'll settle for the bluefish. I've seen it. Many times. I'll see it again, many times, I hope. It alone is wonder enough for me. Compared with all the eccentrics of the salt sea and of land-locked lakes, it's so normal. So noble. It has such an elegant hull. It is wicked and wild when it's hooked. It has such a cruel eye and such passionate jaws. It makes love out in the deep sea, where no peeping-Tom human being will ever pry into its dearest secrets. It's so full of life! And it's true to life; there is nothing fake or soft about it; life is harsh. I've said it before, and I'll say it again: I'm deeply in awe of the bluefish.

—John Hersey, *Blues*

*BLUEFISH*

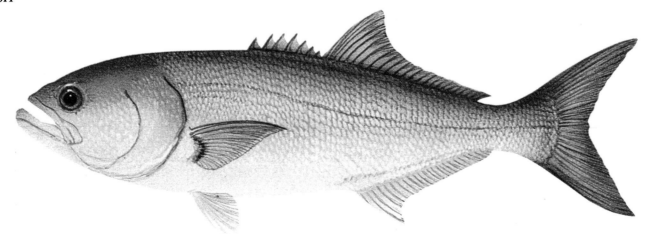

***The bluefish is distributed throughout North Atlantic coastal zones, from the Carolinas to Maine.***

**Range** The bluefish is found in North America off the Atlantic coast, particularly in mid-Atlantic and New England waters from Maine to Newport to Martha's Vineyard and Narragansett to the north Jersey shore. Blues are fairly common as far south as the Carolinas throughout the year. Like many pelagic game fish, bluefish migrate north with warming waters and retreat as temperatures fall in winter. From winter feeding grounds off the southeastern United States, the blues move north and by early summer they reach New York. By July and August, giant schools have settled throughout New England waters as far north as Maine, and some Newfoundland and New Brunswick waters.

One of the mysteries surrounding this most popular of seagoing fish is the reason for the great fluctuations in bluefish population observed around the Atlantic seaboard over the past one hundred years and before. Blues either run in great numbers, as they have recently, or virtually disappear. In *Blues,* John Hersey describes the mystery:

> They were plentiful off the coast of New England in colonial times, but then from about 1764 they totally disappeared and didn't show up again until about 1810. There were tremendous catches from 1880 to about 1905, when they dropped off again for several years. There was a sharp decline again in the forties; in 1941 almost none were caught

except for a few off Maryland and Virginia.... A strange thing is that the abundance cycles of bluefish are reciprocal to those of striped bass; when one species is up, the other's down.

**Color**

In or just out of the water, the bluefish looks like a silvery blue torpedo. The bluegreen cast of the fish's back gathers a bright silver sheen on the flanks and belly. Upon death, the colors fade to light blue-gray.

**Identifying characteristics**

The streamlined body, toothy jaws and notched double dorsal fin make identifying the bluefish fairly easy. A check of the blue's second dorsal fin will reveal a jutting spine. There is a distinct dark blotch at the base of the blue's pectoral fins.

Schools of blues can often be identified slashing through the surface of the water—often close to shore—as they chase baitfish to the surface in a spectacular and voracious feeding frenzy that sends minnows leaping into the air to escape snapping jaws. Seagulls wheel in for easy scavenging as the water slicks with blood and chopped pieces of fish. The plankton (fed on by the minnows, which in turn are fed on by the bluefish) releases an unmistakable smell of melon on the wind. Often blues will drive schools of silversides or menhaden against the beach where they throw themselves onto the sand by the thousands to escape the blues' relentless feeding. And sometimes the blues strand themselves on the sand in aggressive pursuit of the fleeing minnows. Any surf caster privileged enough to witness this spectacle and get a plug in

*A silvery blue torpedo of razor-jawed predatory destruction.*

the water will never forget the fishing that follows. In fact, he or she may come to agree with thousands of others that pound for pound, the bluefish is the greatest fighting sport fish, fresh or saltwater, on the face of the earth.

**Size**

Most anglers will catch blues in the three- to four-pound range, with ten- and twelve-pounders winning the trophies in surf fishing towns during Atlantic seaboard summers. In Africa,

© James D. Watt

*With stripers in decline, the bluefish has become the leading target of saltwater sportfishers in coastal North Atlantic waters. But no species is limitless, and unregulated fishing of the blue will lead to its decline as well.*

blues commonly reach forty pounds, and considering the aggressiveness of the blue, these specimens might give the Great White a fair battle in the ring. The record blue taken in American waters on rod and reel was caught off a pier at Cape Hatteras and weighed thirty-one pounds, twelve ounces. Bluefish from the same school are remarkably similar in size, with no more than an ounce or two separating the largest fish from the smallest.

**Spawning period**

Blues spawn in the open sea from April to August. Individual schools will take two or three weeks to spawn, migrating to deep water at different times over this period, depending on location and water temperature. Some marine biologists speculate that there are two distinct genetic stocks of bluefish, one that spawns in the spring off the Carolinas, and another that spawns from July to August in the waters off the mid-Atlantic and New England seaboards. Ichthyologists and biologists know very little about the mating or courting habits of these fish.

**Angling notes**

Is the bluefish the most savage predator in the sea? Many anglers and ichthyologists think so. No fish eats more often with more voracity, consuming several times its own weight every day. After the water has been bloodied in a major feeding attack, blues will snap at one another in cannibalistic frenzy. Anglers, swimmers, and surfers have been badly bitten by marauding blues. Stories of blue attacks on humans have circulated for years, including the famous story of Navy divers afloat off the coast of North Africa during World War II who were eaten alive by schooling blues "on the feed."

The blue's assertive personality has made it popular among saltwater fishermen all over the Atlantic Coast. The blue is extremely popular prey for the surf caster, but it can be taken in a number of ways—from small boats offshore, on the fly rod from jetties, or from piers and bridges. Surf casters often claim to pick up a pleasant cucumberish or melony smell when blues are running and feeding near the shore: This is in fact the smell of the plankton consumed by the small baitfish that have in turn been consumed by the hungry bluefish.

**Lures**

Many lures are tried, and many catch fish. Classic bluefish lures include pencil poppers like the Gibbs Pencil Popper, M&M Chopper Popper or Atom Spin Atom, large minnow lures from Rapala, Rebel, Sea Hawk, and Red Gill. Feathered jigs, eel skins, tin squids like the Keel Squid and Butterfish Squid, and wobbling spoons such as the Kastmaster will draw plenty of toothy action.

**Bait**

Menhaden and other baitfish or squid strung on a good-sized hook slowly trolled under the surface is the preferred method. Some surf casters use eels or squid. Chumming with ground menhaden is an effective method for drawing bluefish to the surface where the boated angler can cast to them with lighter saltwater spinning gear or even heavy fly tackle.

**Flies**

Bluefish will hit a streamer and, believe me, playing a bluefish on a saltwater fly rod is like dipping your arms into live electricity.

**Best tackle**

Medium-weight saltwater bait-casting or spinning reels and rods provide sufficient power to bring home the blues while giving the fish a chance to show their strength. Often blues are caught on heavy trolling tackle and are cranked aboard by the angler with little fuss. Blues are fierce, fearless, and strong, and will give the surf angler a memorable fight. Light-weight casting or surf-casting tackle is popular among veteran anglers who know that the ferocious blue can give a great battle: Fast-taper six- to eight-foot casting rods with ten-ounce reels and 7- to 10-lb. test make fighting and landing medium-sized blues from a boat a significant challenge. A nine- to ten-foot surf-casting rod with 10-lb. test rigged on a spinning reel is ideal surf weaponry for catching blues in the waves. Any bluefish rig should include a wire leader.

© Allan Weitz

*Medium-weight bait-casting tackle can handle most bluefish. Spinning reels work better for surfcasting.*

# BONEFISH

*As others have wanted to walk on the moon and some have wished to scale Everest, I wanted to catch a bonefish on a fly, an accomplishment I felt was a culmination of the entire art of fly fishing.*

—Charles Waterman, *In Waters Swift and Still*

*BONEFISH*

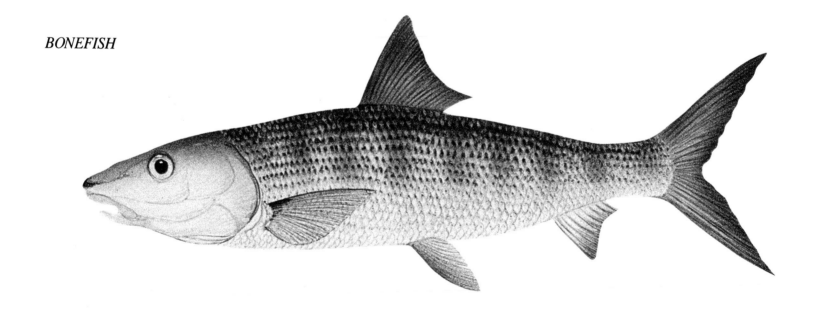

| | |
|---|---|
| **Range** | Bonefish can be found in the coastal and tidal shallows of the Florida Keys and Bahamas, the Antilles and Virgin Islands of the Caribbean, and the coastal waters of Belize, Panama, and other Central American countries. |

| | |
|---|---|
| **Color** | The bonefish is a beautiful creature. The sides and belly are bright, shimmering silver, and its fins and mouth are tinged with soft, golden yellow. |
| **Identifying characteristics** | Bonefish have an armor-plated head and a long piglike snout. They are often |

seen breaking the surface of the water on the flats with their tails as they root in sand for shrimp and crabs. The bonefish has a single dorsal fin with seventeen to nineteen soft rays.

**Size**
A bone caught on rod and reel will average six to eight pounds. Many adults are larger, and ten-pound catches are common. Bonefish swim in schools or smaller pods of five to ten fish, with smaller specimens grouping in larger numbers.

**Spawning period**
Bonefish spawn in open waters in the late spring. Their reproductive habits are not well known. The great angling writer, William Humphrey, wrote "Less is known about the bonefish than any other game fish. What is known sets the bonefish apart as solitary and strange. The bonefish has no close relatives; it is the only member of its family. Unlike most fish, which bury their eggs in the waterbed, bonefish lay eggs which float upon the surface of the water. They broadcast their milt at large upon the surface to find and fertilize the eggs."

The mystery of the bonefish continues when their larval and juvenile growth are examined. The hatchling bonefish looks like an eel, not a bonefish. After a few weeks of growth, when it reaches a size of about three inches, it undergoes a period of metamorphosis during which the hatchling shrinks to half its size. As it shrinks, fins grow and after ten to twelve days, the eelish hatchling has been transformed by nature's mysterious genetic blueprint into a 1- to 1.5-inch miniature bonefish, after which it will grow at a normal rate.

© M. Timothy O'Keefe/Tom Stack & Associates

*The bonefish frequents sandy tidal flats and kelp beds. It is extremely sensitive to disturbances in its environment—and to the presence of anglers. This bonefish, however, has been fooled.*

**Angling notes**
The bonefish is often called the silver streak of the saltwater flats, wandering tidal waters in search of the shrimp, crabs, mussel, and other crustaceans it enjoys. This silver-finned ghost has captured the imagination of anglers the world over. A shy, seemingly intelligent fish, the bonefish is extremely sensitive to its environment, and any unusual noise or disturbance on the flats when the fish is vulnerable will send it rocketing off the flats to safer, less exposed water. Its palate is fussy, and bait or flies must be carefully presented. The bonefish is uncommonly strong for its size; when it is hooked, it can burn off line from a fly or spinning reel like the Tasmanian devil.

A drift or flatboat is essential to bonefishing, as are sunglasses and a pair of old sneakers. Bonefish are stalked from flatboats, and anglers will cast from the boat, or if a closer approach is necessary, wade for them after they have been sighted. Guides are *de rigueur* in bonefishing: Bones are

*The bonefish is a bottom feeder, as indicated by the downward curl of its snout.*

difficult to find and to spot; locating them consistently is a skill acquired over years, not days. Guides pole their boats through the flats noiselessly. Conversation is minimal. Hand signals are used. Dedicated bone fishermen have been known to wade for twenty or thirty yards *on their knees* to make a presentation.

The world's best bonefishing is found in the Florida Keys, Bahamas, and Belize in Central America. The best spots include Chub Cay, Abaco, Andros Island, Eleuthera, Long Island, Crooked Island, and Saint George's Cay in the Bahamas, Biscayne Bay, Key Largo, Islamorada and many other base points for fishing Keys flats.

Bonefish nose in the bottom for shrimp and crustaceans, so any lure, bait, or fly presentation must lay on the bottom where the bone will find it. Guides will look for swirls of mud where the bonefish are digging in the sand for crustaceans and then advise their clients to cast in front of the "mud."

**Lures**  Because the bonefish enjoys relatively recent popularity with tourists and professionals, fish-taking strategies are still in development, and the word is not yet in on many lures and rigs. Flat-bodied jigs like the Wiggle Jig are seeing more use. Anglers and guides have tried soft plastic lures and pork rinds with limited success. Whatever the lure, it is fished this way: After the bonefish is spotted on the flat, the guide will pole into position and the angler will cast a lure to lead the path of the bone's feeding line. The result is one of the most exciting moments in outdoor sport, the

*nudge,* or bump, of a bonefish mouthing the bait, the strike, and that first electrifying run that feels as if it could blow the reel off the rod.

**Bait**  Shrimp is the leader far and away. Crushed crab, skate, mollusk, and clams are favored by some.

**Flies**  The popularity of bonefish among serious fly fishermen is reaching the proportions of cult religion. Fly fishing for bonefish requires the highest levels of skill and stealth. Anglers must be able to cast quickly and accurately to distances of sixty and seventy feet, landing their fly *in front* of the bonefish, not behind, which will spook them. Strikes cannot be seen at this distance, and since the bonefish gently mouths bait, the hook must be set on a quiet tightening or tap of the line. Bonefish must be waded and cast to without the angler being seen. Bonefishermen with fly rods will often approach the bone on their knees as they prepare to cast.

Important bonefish flies include the Pink, White, Yellow, and Tan Moe flies, Marabou Charlies in Yellow, Tan, Green, and White, Bonefish Special, Salt Shrimp, Crayfish, Boneanze, and Crab.

**Best tackle**  For fly fishing, the angler needs a heavy single-action reel that can hold eight- or ten-weight fly line and two hundred yards or so of backing, a nine- to ten-foot fast-taper fly rod, and a long, stout leader. Spinning reels wound with two hundred or so yards of 6- to 10-lb. test, paired with a medium-action saltwater spinning rod will give spin fishermen all the muscle they need.

# COBIA

## (Ling, Lemonfish, Crabeater, Black Salmon)

*N*ow, fishing for cobia—out around those oil derricks—they really tie you up: that's real fishing.

—President George Bush

*COBIA*

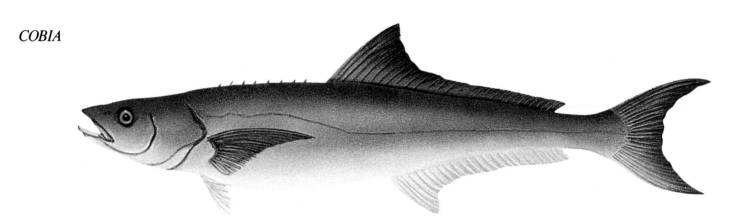

**Range**

The cobia is a streamlined, hard-hitting and hard-running predator in the one-hundred-pound class with a marked predilection for frequenting buoys, wrecks, oil derricks, pilings, anchored boats, and other submerged and floating objects. It is found in warm and tropical waters worldwide but rarely farther north in U.S. waters than Key West and the Gulf coast. Cobia feed on school fish as well as squid, shrimp, crabs, and other crustaceans.

**Color**

The cobia's body is dark chocolate-brown, and the flanks are striped with broad whitish, bronze, or black hori-zontal bands, depending on age and habitat. All fins are also brown, and the cobia's belly is a creamy beige.

**Identifying Characteristics**

The cobia is shaped like a mackerel with a flat head and a concave, fanned tail. Some anglers compare the cobia's appearance to a whiskerless catfish. Angling commentators also point out the striking similarity in appearance and behavior between the cobia and the remora, including their love for hanging out with sharks and rays (undoubtedly to scoop up leftovers and other secondary meals). The cobia can be identified by its matching long second dorsal and anal fins in addition to the set of eight to ten finless spines in its first dorsal.

**Size**

Most adults weigh between forty and seventy-five pounds, but multiyear elders can easily top a hundred pounds. The world record cobia, caught in Australia, scaled out at 135 pounds, nine ounces.

**Spawning period**

According to Charles Waterman in a 1980 article in *Saltwater Sportsman*, it is suspected that cobia spawn between May and June in the Gulf of Mexico, and between July and August in the late-warming Chesapeake Bay and northeastern Atlantic. Spawning generally takes place in the open oceans, where millions of eggs are dispersed. Adult cobia remain off-shore to feed until fall, but the young cobia hatchlings migrate in-shore immediately to feed in the nutrient-rich coastal and surf zones.

**Angling notes**

The cobia is an omnivorous feeder who will forage the nooks and crannies of favored habitats—offshore buoys, oil derricks, lighthouses, and wrecks, as well as riptides and flotsam—from bottom to top (more frequently on the bottom) for crabs, fish (particularly flounder), squid, and scraps. Cobia will move inshore occasionally and can be caught from piers and jetties if the water isn't too shallow. This is all good news for anglers because cobia are susceptible to the gamut of saltwater fishing methods.

Cobia fight well, making long runs and laps, diving for the bottom, or racing toward the boat in unpredictable patterns. They are respected game fish that get less publicity than other fish because their habitat makes them difficult to land once hooked.

Try casting around buoys, oil rigs, and wrecks with large plugs and baits to catch prowling cobia; they are aggressive predators and will almost always take a shot at a "wounded" baitfish. Trolling is effective close to offshore structures at five to six miles per hour with heavier 6/0 to 7/0 boat tackle and heavy wire terminal rigs. Wire leaders are necessary when cobia fishing close to offshore structures, because once it is hooked a cobia will dive for cover, and it takes a lot of leverage to get it out. Bottom fishing in cobia habitats will probably yield the most fish, though it inevitably also means catching a few "undesirables."

**Lures**

Large Johnson or Eppinger saltwater spoons or any sort of darting plugs.

**Bait**

Cobia enjoy cut flounder, small live flounder, live or cut mullet, and squid, shrimp, or crab.

**Best tackle**

Lighter tackle is best for bottom fishing, except around heavy structures: The cobia's initial bites or takes can be faint and you won't need stiff-butted rods or big boat reels to land it. Try 20-lb. test on a lightweight to medium-weight spinning rod with light action and a large casting or spinning reel with capacity for at least 250 yards of line. If the cobia are breaking off on structure add a wire leader, and if they continue to succeed try heavier tackle. Jigging can also be very profitable in cobia hunts. Chumming will, as always, increase the odds of catching large numbers of fish.

# JACK CREVALLE

## (Toro, Cavally, Horse Crevalle)

*T*he most breathtaking moments in our morning walks came when jack crevalle suddenly rushed out of the channels to drive schools of mullet up against the sea wall where they could not escape. Time and again the mullet leaped desperately against the wall until its rough surface and barnacles had completely scaled the most energetic among them.

—George Rieger, *Wanderer on My Native Shore*

*JACK CREVALLE*

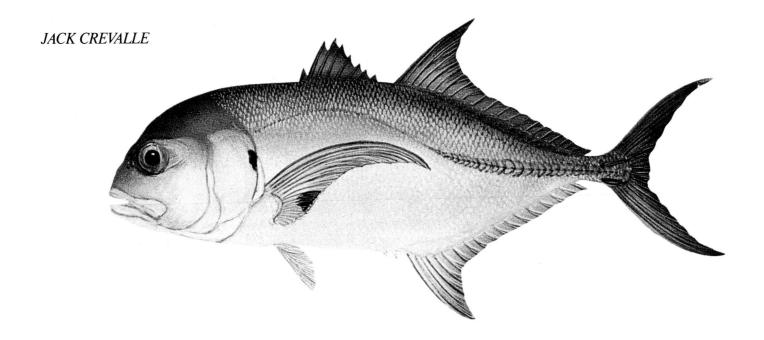

**Range** The jack crevalle is a supremely strong light-tackle inshore game fish that schools in the warm waters of the Atlantic, from the northeastern United States to South America. The crevalle is most common in the inshore zones and reef waters of Florida, the Keys, the Bahamas, and the Gulf of Mexico. The Pacific species is heavily distributed through the subtropical and temperate coastal seas of southern California, Baja, and Hawaii. Schools of crevalle frequent tidal bays and channels, inlets, offshore reefs, edge water, and channels of harbors and bays, as well as the salt-water flats. Their predilection for ascending brackish rivers after bait species is well known.

**Color** The crevalle's back is a glittering metal-lic bluegreen and it is striped with buttery yellow on the flanks. The lower half of the fish is ivory.

**Identifying characteristics** The crevalle is a common warm-water game fish easily distinguished by its squared-off forehead and paired dorsal fins set more than half-way back on the fish's body. However, to distinguish the crevalle from its first cousin, the horse-eye jack, look at the chest. The chest of the horse-eye jack is completely covered in scales but the crevalle's chest bears only a small scaly patch. Only the crevalle wears a distinct black spot or blotch on the pectoral fin and another on the gill flap.

**Size** Crevalle are common in weights of eight to ten pounds and easily found at fifteen and twenty pounds. They begin to thin out at the top of the growth ladder above twenty-five pounds. A thirty-

*The crevalle gives unrelenting battle for its size. Fifteen and twenty-pounders are common.*

five-pound crevalle is a trophy. The IGFA world record is a 57-pound, 5-ounce jack caught off Barra do Kwanza, Angola, in 1992.

**Spawning period** Jack crevalle spawn between March and September in off-shore waters, ichthyologists now generally agree. In warmer tropical and sub-tropical waters, spawning begins earlier in spring; farther north on the Atlantic and Pacific coasts, the crevalle wait until summer before

© Norbert Wu

*Jack crevalle frequent Atlantic and Pacific warm water reefs where juvenile and adult fish travel in schools.*

spawning. A.J. McClane has written that early reports of biologists describing in-shore crevalle spawning have been disproven by field observations in the last decade.

**Angling notes** One of the great light-tackle saltwater game fish, the crevalle is respected for its fighting abilities that can keep an angler engaged in battle for an hour with a ten- or fifteen-pound fish. Schools of crevalle wander over tropical Atlantic and Pacific warm-water reefs and flats. When found, they are among the surest bets for the boat-ready light-tackle saltwater angler. Crevalles slash and chase through the waves, herding bait fish that are swimming in formerly calm pieces of ocean into agitated schools, on which the crevalles feed rapaciously. When crevalle are hot on the feed, they'll hit anything. This is most definitely *not* bonefishing.

Other jacks popular with sport fishermen include the blue runner, amberjack, and horse-eye jack. The amberjack is a wide-ranging predator found feeding on the surface during migration, though its natural habitat is near reef bottoms, shelves, and seawalls where currents swirl to form holes and gullies that attract baitfish in huge numbers.

© Daniel W. Gotshall

**Pacific amberjack**

They range throughout warm eastern and western Atlantic and Pacific waters. Amberjack are the frequent target of boat-tackle trollers, who ply the species with slowly dragged deep-running lures, spoons, plugs, jigs, or strip baits. Bait fishing is highly popular in catching amberjack, with pinfish, grunts, mullet, and other small fish the favored offerings. Amberjack hit hard, run deep, and fight with the power of a freight train. They reach huge sizes in the hundreds of pounds.

**Bait**  Menhaden, silversides, balao, and mullet will work just fine when they are cast into a feeding school of crevalle.

**Best tackle**  Crevalle are muscular fish with extraordinary strength for their size, which means they can't be angled too finely on light saltwater tackle. A medium-weight, eight- to nine-foot medium- to light-action bait-casting rod fitted with 15- to 20-lb. test and a solid bait-casting reel will keep matters exciting while providing the muscle you'll need when the toro bursts off on its third or fourth surge, stripping your spool to the bone. A school of crevalle can run you ragged, so you'll want durable tackle that keeps you in the ring fight after fight.

# DOLPHIN

**(Also called *mahi-mahi* in Hawaii, *sūra* in Japan, and *dorado* in Central America.)**

*There seems to be no satisfying the ravenous appetite of dolphinfish. I have seen them snatch baits just a few inches in front of the noses of big sharks and billfish. At first sight of a tobogganing bait, this voracious creature, like the needlefish, often takes off from a great distance and comes bounding through the air, or rips the surface for a hundred yards to be first at the morsel. When hooked, it bounds as high as 15 feet. I know of no other 50- to 75-pound swimmer that will hit a lure trolled at 20 knots and pass the boat before the angler can feel the strike, then keep the rod in the form of a question mark for an hour and a half.*

—Ray Cannon, *The Sea of Cortez*

*DOLPHIN (Male)*

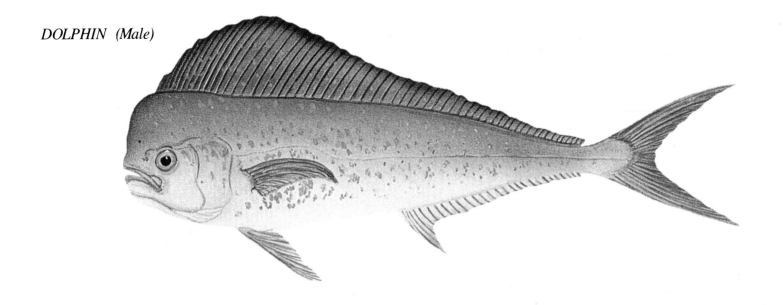

*DOLPHIN (Female)*

**Identifying characteristics**

Male dolphin are distinguished by a bluntly angled, axe-shaped head, but the female's head follows a smoother, gracefully rounded curve into the body. Their tails are dramatically forked and their long dorsal fins begin behind the head and end slightly above the tail. Dolphin can be distinguished from their first cousin, the pompano, by their dorsal fin, which begins immediately behind the head, as opposed to the pompano's, which begins in the middle of the spine. The pompano is also fatter and less colorful than the dolphin.

**Size**

Dolphin grow at an extraordinary metabolic rate, gaining weight and size with unbelievable speed. Most reach peak maturity within a year, and die within four years. Dolphin grow at a rate of three to five pounds a month. The small schooling dolphin that draw the attention of thousands of anglers in the Gulf of Mexico or off the California Baja are usually no more than two or three months old; dolphin in the seventy- or eighty-pound world-record class were found to be no more than four years old. Captive dolphin have grown to weights of thirty-five to forty-pounds in less than eight months. This extraordinary fish lives hard and dies young— as dolphin anglers will attest.

Young dolphin mature and spawn within their first year, reaching lengths of eighteen inches or more. Most anglers will catch the small two- to five-pound schooling dolphin that attack any and all lures and baits with reckless abandon. Larger and less frequently spotted fish will run between five and ten pounds, and any boated dolphin tilting the scales over twenty pounds is a distinguished catch. The present IGFA world record is an eighty-seven-pound dolphin caught in the Papagallo Gulf, Costa Rica, in 1976.

**Spawning period**

Dolphin spawn from late winter through summer off southern Florida, with peak activity from January through March. Dolphin born early in the year will probably spawn later that same year in the fall.

**Angling notes**

The dolphin is a favorite saltwater sport fish, easily available in relatively shallow flats and open water off northern, central, and southern Florida, the Bahamas, the Caribbean, the Gulf of Mexico, and Baja, and throughout the southern Pacific. A relentless and enthusiastic feeder, the compliant dolphin hits lures and baits of all kinds with blinding speed, often nabbing three or four trolled menhaden or balao before the angler sets the hook. Dolphin are believed to swim at speeds of up to fifty miles per hour. Although it is not as strong as the tarpon, or able to leap as high as the sailfish, or nearly as tough as the tuna or amberjack, the dolphin fights angler, line, and hook with everything it's got.

A seven- or eight-foot saltwater spinning rod fitted with a fairly light bait-casting reel and 20-lb. test makes for more than enough tackle power to face larger dolphin. The challenge really begins at 12- or 10-lb. test which is still perfectly adequate, if not too easy, for many of the smaller school dolphin, but very tricky when fighting 20- and 30-pound fish. The dolphin is perhaps the most challenging and satisfying ocean fish to land on light tackle, a trickster of blazing speed and ingenuity. It will hurl itself into the air repeatedly, sometimes as high as twenty feet, attempting to throw the hook; it will run straight at the boat, running up slack on the line, then change direction, jumping again and again, its colorful coat shimmering in the sun; it will dodge and jump until completely drained of energy.

**Dolphin are among the most popular sportfish in the Baja.**

Provided the tackle is light, anglers who boat a dolphin have earned that next cold can of beer.

Dolphin have a curious behavioral habit that has puzzled ichthyologists for decades. Individual fish and schools will group under floating debris, seaweed, or driftwood on the open sea, enjoying the cool shadow, protection, and company for days at a time. Veteran captains and professional anglers will often search out large chunks of flotsam and troll or cast through the area. The result is often a strike. Japanese commercial fishermen will build rafts in the open ocean, wait a few days and then return to harvest the dolphin that have gathered beneath.

Whether a professional, beginner, or salty sea dog, a dolphin fisherman need remember only one principle: The dolphin is a swift, open-water fish attracted to swift-swimming prey. It loves a challenge. Fast trolling and casting will draw the dolphin's interest, and when it is interested, it acts quickly.

*A brilliantly colored fish when living—striped with green, yellow, blue, and white and covered with brilliant gold flecks—the dolphin's colors fade to gray and green after death.*

**Lures** Surface poppers like the Arbogast Hammerhead, deep running Rapalas, plastic squid such as the Li'l Octopus or Chummin' Squid, big spoons and spinners—fished at or just below the surface—are all effective. Drone or Johnson spoons often bag plenty of fish. A number of special skimming or skating dolphin "bird" lures, common around southern Florida and the Keys, are easily found in any tackle shop.

**Bait** Trolled mullet, mackerel, squid, or balao will draw the interest of these metabolic furnaces when they're hungry, which is most of the time.

**Flies** Schools brought close to the boat can be fished with a fly rod. While it is well known that catching a dolphin and trailing it about forty feet behind the boat will draw groups of dolphin, most fly fishers would consider this extremely cruel and unsportsmanlike.

**Best tackle** Use a heavy spinning rod, seven feet or so long, carrying 12- or 20-lb.-test line on a casting reel or very heavy spinning reel, or suit up with 20-lb. IFGA boat tackle. An 80- to 100-lb. test mono or coated wire shock leader is recommended for these sharp-toothed fish.

# RED DRUM

## (Channel Bass, Redfish, Bullred, Ratred, Puppy Red)

*What the striped bass is to anglers from the Chesapeake Bay*

*northward, the red drum is to those from there southward.*

—Joseph D. Bates, *Fishing*

*RED DRUM*

**Range**

One of the great shallow-water game fish of North America, red drum are found from Cape Cod to the Florida Everglades and Keys and in Texas along the Gulf Coast and in Galveston Bay and Laguna Madre. The "channel bass" is the leading surf-casting fish of North Carolina's Outer Banks during late spring and early fall, when migrating schools run through inlets and surf zones.

**Color**

"The coppery warrior of the tides" has a red-bronze upper back and wears a distinct black spot on the caudal peduncle. Its lower flanks are an iridescent silvery gray, fading to white on the belly.

**Identifying characteristics**

The red drum can be identified by its coppery brown-red coloration, and it differs from the black drum in its lack of chin barbels. The drum can be easily identified by the round black spot, about the size of its eye, found above the tail on the caudal peduncle. The red

drum's snout is conical, and it has a downward curling mouth.

**Size** Larger fish are often called bulls or bullreds, and commonly weigh fifteen to forty pounds, and sometimes even more. The puppy drum that make up a large part of the red drum fishery in Florida saline and brackish waters rarely weigh more than ten pounds. Twenty-pound bulls are common catches during the highly popular fall runs along the Outer Banks and Virginia and southeastern U.S. coasts. The world-record red drum caught on rod and reel was landed in 1984 at Avon, North Carolina. It weighed 94 pounds, 2 ounces.

**Spawning period** April to September, offshore.

**Angling notes** Surf casting for red drum is a fanatic matter for Outer Banks anglers. Armed with long rods and riding in dune buggies over the sands in search of schools of surf drum running through channels out to sea, or prowling the shallows for crustaceans or plentiful baitfish, the surf casters regard the drum as the premier mid-Atlantic surf-casting game fish, and no one has ever changed the mind of a committed Hatteras Channel

© Lloyd Poissenot

*Smaller "puppy drum" of ten pounds and under are a mainstay of inland and estuary fisheries in southern Florida and the Gulf of Mexico.*

bass angler on this point. The drum also attract armies of anglers on the Gulf coast and in the tidal waters and flats of Florida. Around the Outer Banks, drum fishing peaks with runs of large fish in April and November. Oregon Inlet, Ocracoke, Hatteras, Drum Inlet, Topsail, and Morehead City are some prime Outer Banks locales during hot drum rums. Buxton Point on Hatteras Island, the sloughs ten miles north of the lighthouse at the Cape, and the north shore of Hatteras Inlet have been the hottest waters of all in recent years. The serious drum surf caster will need a dune buggy to get to the fish because roads don't service many of the best spots. If you don't own a dune buggy, you can rent one.

The hundreds of miles of coastal waters from Virginia to South Carolina also offer fine red drum fishing when the bulls are in season.

Although a guide can steer the novice to the channels and gullies where drum are likely to gather to feed near shore, his or her job is finished at that point. Fishing for drum is fairly straightforward, and guides will often go a day or two without finding any. Professional help will improve the odds for the first- or second-timer, but after that surf casters may wish to test their own skills at reading water, following tides, and gathering intelligence on drum schools. The Gulf Coast, Galveston Bay, and the waters of Laguna Madre in Texas offer some of the best drum fishing in the world. In Florida waters, the tidal rivers around the Everglades, Florida Bay, Punta Rassa, Sanibel Island, and Captiva Pass form hundreds of miles of premium drum water. The Ten Thousand Island area is a drum nursery where vast numbers of drum school and feed.

**Lures**

Surf casting requires some work, but virtually without exception the first strike by a bull red melting line from the reel and surging through the surf with throbbing runs and surges will convert the angler to surf casting for life. However, it is largely a bottom-fishing affair, since red drum love to nose and burrow in the sand for crustaceans and other live goodies. When drum are actively herding and feeding on baitfish, however, tin squids, spoons, and plugs will draw immediate strikes. Ten- to twelve-foot fast-taper surf-casting rods, fitted with surf-spinning or large capacity casting reels and 150 to 200 yards of 12- to 15-lb. test are the basic weapons.

**Bait**

For bottom fishing with shrimp, clams, mullet fillet, worms, or crab, a two- or three-once pyramid sinker and 6/0 or 8/0 hooks are required because larger drum with their sinewy mouths require larger-than-usual hooks. When the angler can't see any fish, jigs, plugs, feathers, and spoons are always worth a try, but they must be retrieved slowly. Red drum can also be caught on a variety of fly patterns, including streamers and shrimp imitations.

**Best tackle**

Red drum run smaller in the Gulf and around Florida. Here they are challenging adversaries on light tackle. Try casting small jigs and spoons around oyster beds, mangrove banks, inlets, and tidal river basins. A light spinning outfit with 5- to 8-lb. test provides all the backbone the red drummer needs for the smaller Florida specimens.

# ATLANTIC AND PACIFIC HALIBUT

**Range**

Pacific halibut are found throughout the cold waters of the North Pacific from the Bering Sea to Northern California, and adults are highly migratory, often ranging over thousands of miles of ocean. This highly popular food and game fish prefers deep water, often living in ocean habitats hundreds and even thousands of feet deep.

The Atlantic halibut inhabits cold and deep ocean reaches of the North Atlantic in a range that spans the Barents Sea to the open seas off Virginia.

Both species of this massive flatfish live on the sea bottom and seldom enter shallow water except as freshly hatched youngsters, when they will forage inshore for a few years before moving to the deeps.

**Color**

The Pacific halibut are colored similarly to the Atlantic species, dark brown or gray on top and white on the bottom. Some Atlantic halibut have slightly red or pinkish bellies.

**Identifying characteristics**

The Atlantic halibut has a large mouth that extends to the middle of the eye, while the Pacific halibut has a smaller set of jaws. Both species are equipped with a full set of teeth. Both of those big halibut have concave tails, and their dorsal and anal fins have pointed middle rays.

*Pacific halibut are the largest of the flatfish species, growing to hundreds of pounds.*

© Steve Kraseman/Valan Photos

© Ruth Fairall

**Size**    Prize specimens grow to remarkable, even staggering sizes. The Pacific halibut is the largest Pacific flatfish, and females can reach weights of 500 pounds and nine or ten feet in length. The Atlantic Rabbit variation grows even larger, reaching weights of 800 or 900 pounds.

**Spawning period**    The Atlantic and Pacific halibut spawn in winter, on deep sea bottoms.

**Angling notes**    Adult Atlantic and Pacific halibut feed on fish, skates, crabs, mussels, lobsters, and clams, and also enjoy squid and worms. Any of these baits drifted near the bottom where halibut dwell may draw attention.

**Tackle**    Short heavy-butted deep-sea fiberglass rods with AFTCO rollers and heavy duty baitcasting reels are the tools of the day when cranking hundreds of pounds of halibut from the bottom. Most captains will use 50-pound test line at least, and many will go higher to 70-or 80-lb. Most halibut catches fall under one hundred pounds, but heavy tackle is still necessary.

Atlantic halibut are particularly vigorous fighters and landing a large one can be an all-day affair. Most halibut fishing takes place in cold water and cold weather: wear warm and waterproof clothing and make sure your boat captain has plenty of hot cocoa and coffee available.

# MACKEREL

## (King, Cero, Spanish)

*SPANISH MACKEREL*

**Range**   The king, Spanish, and cero mackerel are highly popular game fish in all waters of the Atlantic. They are swift, aggressive predators that school in large numbers and engage in wide feeding sessions just under the waves. This makes them particularly vulnerable to the oceangoing angler in a party boat.

The king mackerel is a highly migratory fish. Kingfish school throughout tropical and subtropical waters from the coasts of Virginia and Maryland to Brazil. They like to prowl shore waters, tidal rivers, and other freshwater and saltwater interstices more than other mackerel, but will also feed in deep water as they work reefs, buoys, wrecks, and other complex structures where meals are abundant. Only the largest individual fish travel alone.

The spanish mackerel is a warm-water fish that favors the southeastern coastal waters of the United States, the Gulf of Mexico, and northern Caribbean waters around the Yucatan. They travel widely, and from time to time will sweep inshore or into a bay for a day or two of chasing baitfish.

Cero mackerel travel much the same waters as these other top-rated game fish, although they rarely move north of Florida. They are most abundant in the shimmering turquoise waters of the Florida Keys.

**Color**   The king mackerel is generic game fish in color—dark blue-green and on the back, fading to silvery flanks and a white belly.

The Spanish is the most striking of the mackerel, with an irregular shower of golden and yellow-brown spots sprayed on its flanks and a back of iridescent blue-green. The pelvic and anal fin edges are tinged in white; the other fin margins are coated in yellow. The belly is silver.

The cero is similar in color to its Spanish relative but is marked with distinct dark yellow stripes running from head to tail.

**Identifying characteristics**

The action can be fast and furious when a sport-fishing boat hits a school of mackerel, and plenty of fish may be brought aboard. Despite the excitement, most anglers still want to know what individual species they're catching. The king mackerel can be distinguished from other warm-water Atlantic mackerel by the sharp dip in the lateral line below the second dorsal fin, as opposed to the gradually arched lateral line of the cero and Spanish. King mackerel do not show the yellow-and-gold spotting of other tropical mackerel, nor do they have scales on their pectoral fins. The dorsal fin of the king is edged in black. The cero and Spanish fish can most easily be distinguished from each other by watching for gold and yellow stripes on the flanks: Cero have them and Spanish do not.

**Size**

The king mackerel is the largest of this group, averaging eight to ten pounds. A significant number of forty- to sixty-

*Huge schools of mackerel are an easy mark for party boat anglers.*

*Those who would catch king mackerel in the Northeast Atlantic should look for schools of baitfish. The kings will often be nearby.*

pound fish are brought aboard year-round. The world record is a ninety-pounder taken in 1976 in Key West, Florida. The Spanish mackerel will reach fifteen pounds at most, and anglers usually catch two- to five-pound fish. The world record for this light-tackle game fish is a twelve-pound specimen caught off Fort Pierce, Florida. The cero mackerel is of similar proportions to its look-alike cousin.

The world-record catch for cero was a 17-pound, 2-ounce Islamorada beauty captured in 1986.

**Spawning period**

The extremely prolific mackerel species spawn in the open ocean during late spring and early summer, depositing millions of eggs that will float free in the ocean until hatching.

**Angling notes**

Mackerel are plentiful, hungry, and

*Mackerel are a blast on light tackle.*

entirely near the surface, are commonly seen "balling" baitfish schools into tightly swimming groups through which the mackerel then tear in voracious feeding sessions. In such encounters the angler enjoys one of the best light-tackle fishing situations possible on the seas. A bucktail, nylon jig, or swiftly retrieved plug cast with a lightweight saltwater spinning rod and reel will draw instant, electrifying hits and up to twenty minutes or so of frenetic battle. Another cast will bring another fight, until the school is gone. Spanish mackerel are not tarpon, but they could put a five-pound Montana rainbow on a towrope and drag it around for hours.

Cero and Spanish as well as king mackerel sometimes move into flats or tidal areas after fleeing baitfish, and here the bonefish or tarpon hunter of the flats can pick up some easy action.

**Best tackle** King mackerel are often found deeper than other warm-water mackerel, up to forty feet underwater where they hang out near wrecks, seawalls, and reefs. Slow trolling with light tackle of the 5/0 to 6/0 class with deep running plugs, rubber squid, or strip or live baits is the choice method when the kingfish are working the depths. Should the angler's taste run to top-water casting or trolling, chumming with shrimp can often bring up a nearby school. But top-water schools of large kingfish on the hunt are far from uncommon. With a little navigational skill from the boat's captain, anglers can catch some hefty specimens with medium-weight spinning or casting tackle—or even trolling gear for those who'd like to drink as much beer as possible before catching fish.

very active game fish, which makes them wonderfully good sport for casual saltwater anglers. There are as many methods for catching mackerel at various depths as can be invented. These fish are not picky: When mackerel are located, jigs, plugs, live and strip baits, and even flies and streamers will draw their attention.

**Lures** Spanish and cero, feeding almost

# MARLIN

'What's that?' she asked a waiter and pointed to the long backbone of the great fish that was now just garbage waiting to go out with the tide.

'Tiburon,' the waiter said. 'Eshark.' He was meaning to explain what had happened.

'I didn't know sharks had such handsome, beautiful fully formed tails.'

'I didn't either,' her male companion said.

—Ernest Hemingway, *The Old Man and The Sea*

BLUE MARLIN *(Atlantic female)*

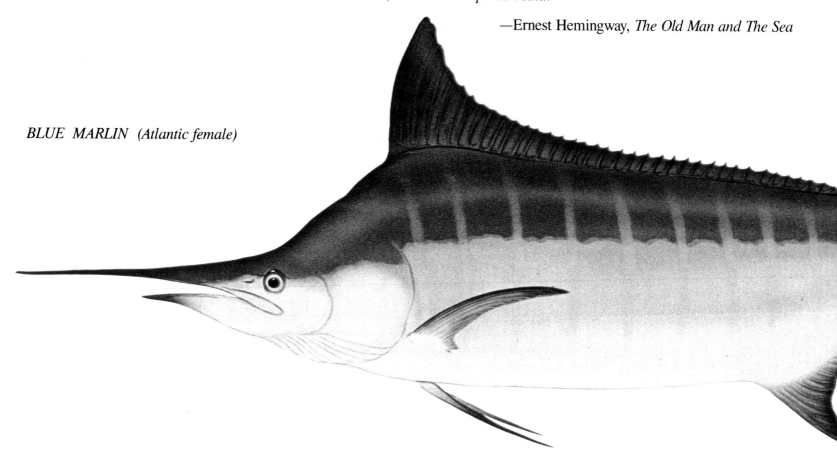

*BLUE MARLIN (Pacific male)*

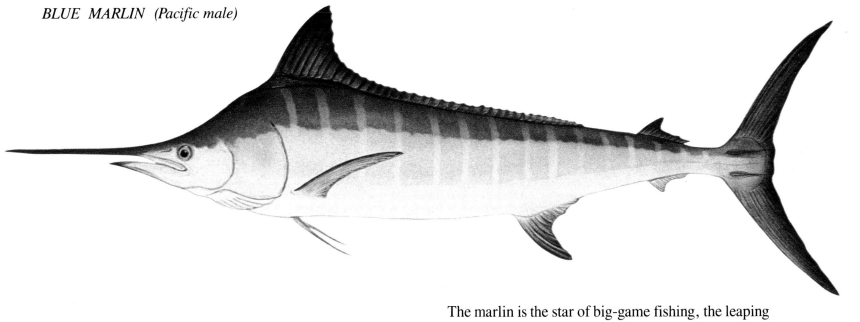

The marlin is the star of big-game fishing, the leaping eagle-billed battler of literature and legend. It is also the customary "trophy" carcass hung by chains with white numbers painted on its belly, seen in fishing magazines and office-wall photos. It is the ultimate prize for the study walls of the wealthy, the longed-for object of thousands of deep-sea expeditions on big boats with flying bridges and huge downriggers.

Hemingway loved the marlin, wrote about it, and set the tone for post-war generation high rollers. Business executives and other open-water afficionados fly to Cat Cay, Bahamas, Bimini, Hawaii, and other tropical locales and pony up significant dollars in hopes of latching onto one of these spectacular billed eagles of the ocean. If a typical high roller gets a hookup, he or she will spend five or six hours or more of back-breaking, arm-numbing labor cranking the marlin to the boat—and may still lose it. If he or she does land the beast, the fish will usually be killed. The victorious angler will probably explain that after the exhaustion and struggle of the long fight with a powerful fish, it is psychologically necessary to make the kill, lest the entire experience fall short of satisfaction. Most blue-water anglers would agree that the the marlin is a graceful, beautiful predator that inspires respect—yet, they still insist upon killing it. With the IGFA's introduction of tag-and-release contests and other inducements to encourage the release of these magnificent creatures, as well as general recognition among anglers that these animals should be preserved, this situation has improved greatly.

**Range**   The white marlin ranges throughout the Atlantic from Venezuela through the Bahamas, the Virgin Islands, and the Florida Keys up to Massachusetts, shifting in constant migration from one region to the next. Whites also occur in the Mediterranean.

Striped marlin are strictly Pacific born and bred, ranging from Chile northward to Baja and southern California. They congregate in feeding grounds near Japan, Hawaii, Fiji, Korea, Formosa, Tahiti, and other southern Pacific and Pacific Rim coastal regions. The Pacific black marlin is native to all tropical waters of the Pacific and Indian Oceans.

The blue marlin is the most widely distributed of the family. It has been caught all over the world. Blue marlin are generally divided for the sake of record keeping into Pacific and Atlantic blues, but no biological difference exists between these fish except in the lateral line: Pacific blue marlin have a lateral line shaped in loops like a chain; the Atlantic blue's lateral line is a more complex reticulated network of hexagonal shapes. Atlantic blues are concentrated in tropical waters; they congregate in large numbers around Bimini, the Bahamas, Puerto Rico, Havana, and off Texas in the Gulf of Mexico. They flock heavily to the Tongue of the Ocean, a deep ocean bank off the Bahamas. A number of world records have been taken around the Virgin Islands and British West Indies. Blue marlin are known to run around Puerto Rico and the Bahamas each June, but they are also present in large numbers between early July and early August. Blue marlin are hotly pursued off Hawaii throughout the spring and summer.

**Color**   White marlin are slender, spear-shaped fish with round, spotted dorsal fins and curved pectoral fins. Their backs are steel gray with a wash of blue, and the lower flanks are white and feature light blue bars that run horizontally from back to belly.

Striped marlin are so named because stripes appear on their bodies after they are dead. Their backs are dark steely blue brightening to blue-silver flanks and fading to white below the lateral line.

© Tim Choate

*Boating a three or four hundred pound marlin such as this white is dangerous business. To release such a beautiful specimen is an act of moral responsibility.*

BLACK MARLIN (Male)

STRIPED MARLIN

WHITE MARLIN

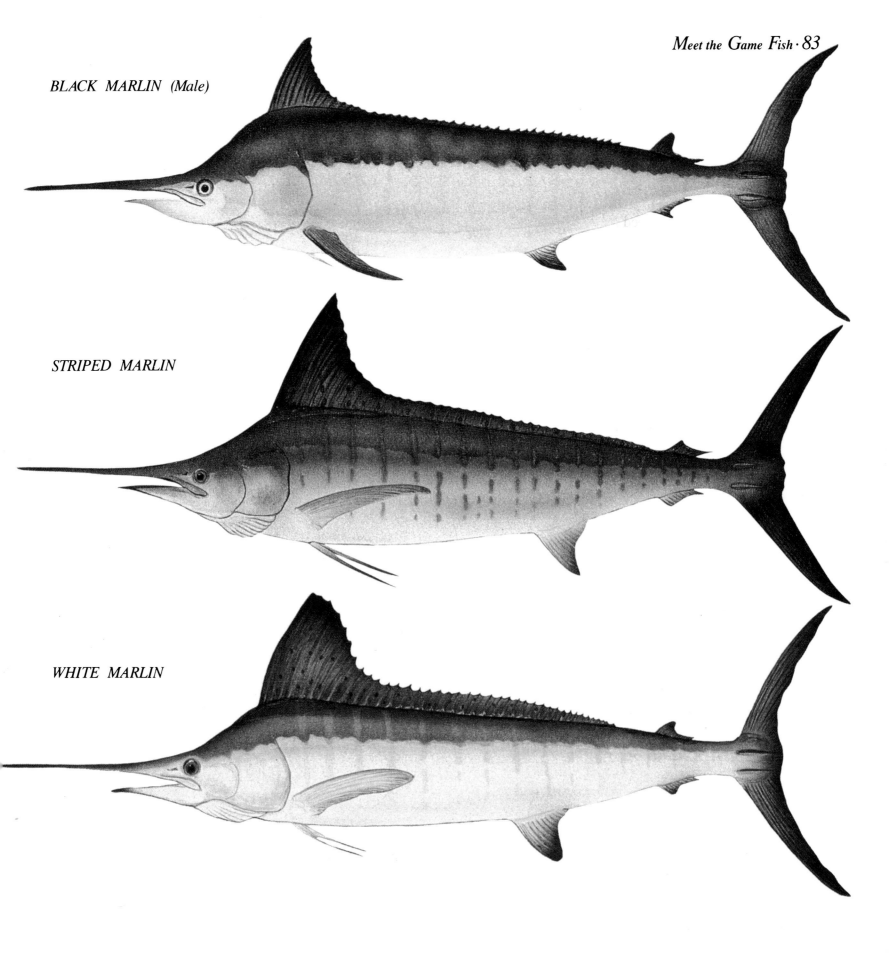

Black marlin are dark slate blue above the lateral line, silvery white below. Light blue stripes are visible in some fish, as is the occasional silvery tone that causes Hawaiians and others to call the fish silver marlin.

Blue marlin wear deep smoky blue or dark brown on the back, lightening to white on the belly. They are marked with thin, light blue horizontal pinstripes. All marlins have long, thin scales, a huge forked tail balanced by a pair of keel fins at the read of the body, as well as the unmistakable bill.

**Identifying characteristics**

Detailed study not possible on the open seas may be necessary to distinguish various marlin species; individual fish may be almost identical in color and size but of different species. Nevertheless, here are some guideposts to keep in mind.

The white marlin has rounded (not pointed as in other marlin) pectoral, dorsal, and anal fins. The black marlin's body is narrower than other species, and the shorter neutral fins never exceed twelve inches. The first dorsal fin is the shortest of any billfish, less

*Striped marlin*

© James D. Watt

*A big-game Penn or Daiwa reel with a superb drag mechanism is essential if the angler is to have a fighting chance against adult marlin.*

than half of the marlin's body depth.

The high, pointed first dorsal fin of the striped marlin is larger than in any other marlin species and can exceed the body depth of the fish. The striper has a straight, highly visible lateral line. No fish in the ocean will jump as often and as high as the striped marlin once hooked.

The blue marlin's dorsal fin is high and pointed, not rounded, and it is relatively shallow in comparison to the body. Lateral line is complex: looped on the Pacific marlin, hexagonal on the Atlantic.

**Size**    The white marlin averages around sixty to seventy pounds per specimen, and the rod-and-reel world-record white weighed 161 pounds when brought to the dock in the Gulf Stream off Miami Beach in 1938. The most abundant of these species, the striped marlin, belongs in the middle-heavyweight division, usually tipping the scales at two or three hundred pounds, with four-hundred-pounders rare, but not earth-shakingly so. The world record striper was nailed off Balboa, California, in the 1940s at 692 pounds. The blue and black marlin rank among the mightiest boned fish in the ocean, with females of the species often exceeding a thousand

pounds. The all-tackle world-record black marlin weighing 1,560 pounds was taken off Cabo Blanco, Peru, in 1953. The all-tackle Atlantic blue marlin world record is a 1,402-pound, 2-ounce fish caught off Vitoria, Brazil, in 1992; the Pacific blue world record is a 1,376-pound fish caught off Kona, Hawaii, in 1982. Perhaps more money is spent by sport fisherman catching these fish than any other on earth. The average blue marlin caught by open-water sport fisherman will weigh between three and four hundred pounds, although many heftier specimens are brought to the gaff.

**Spawning period**

All marlin spawn in spring or summer in the open ocean; the striper spawns in southern Pacific waters off the Baja in midsummer; the white marlin spawns in spring between April and May.

**Angling notes**

Marlin are the supreme predators of the sea. You can't jig for a marlin, cast to it with cute Rapala plugs, run a spinner by its nose, or skitter a streamer fly over its hold. To catch a marlin's attention, you must have a sizable and seemingly alive baitfish, squid, or counterfeit and move it over the ocean's surface at a good clip. This requires trolling with big-game tackle, outriggers, and a first mate. Favorite trolling baits include flying strip bait, mullet mackerel, balao, bonito, herring, and flying fish (or whatever other species are available locally and known to the marlin.) Whatever bait is chosen, the fish's body must be able to hold up to high-speed trolling. Konahead, Mold Craft High Speeds and Soft Birds, Boone Teasers, Seven Strand Minnoclones, Tony Accetta Jelly Bellys, Doorknobs, and other right-speed trolling lures are *de rigueur* with most blue water captains. Among the best places to catch marlin in North America are Cape Hatteras, North Carolina, for blues; Ocean City, Maryland, for whites; the Tongue of the Ocean off the Bahamas for blues and whites; Destin City, Florida, for blues and whites; Catalina, Santa Rosa, San Clemente, and Santa Cruz Islands off southern California for stripers; the Sea of Cortez

*This shimmering striper was hooked near Kealakekua, Hawaii.*

off Baja for stripers, and occasionally black marlin.

Marlin can also be taken on flies, though this is rather difficult.

**Best tackle**

High-powered boat tackle with thirty- to one hundred thirty-pound rods and lever-drag reels, braided line, and wire leader.

Perhaps nothing compares in angling to seeing a thousand-pound fish leap fifteen feet in the air, shaking its head violently to dislodge the hook as its ten-foot body cartwheels in the air to crash against the water. Nothing in angling is as physically challenging as bringing such a fish to the gaff. And nothing in angling takes as much moral courage as releasing that extraordinary predator to live and fight again.

*The blue marlin has few enemies in the sea, and thus may reach sizes of over 1,000 pounds.*

# PERMIT

## (Florida or Mexican or Great Pompano)

*N*o form of fishing offers such elaborate silences as fly-fishing for permit. The most successful permit fly-fisherman in the world has very few catches to describe to you. Yet there is considerable agreement that taking a permit on a fly is the extreme experience of the sport.

—Thomas McGuane, *An Outside Chance*

*PERMIT*

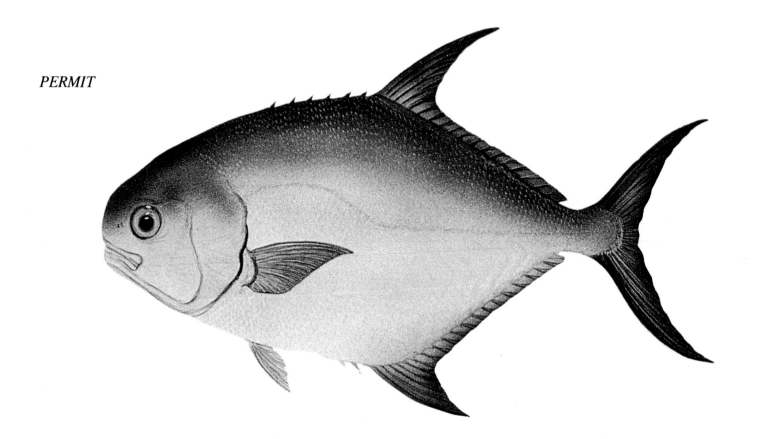

**Range**    The permit lives in the western tropical Atlantic, frequenting the flats and channels around the Florida Keys from Miami to Tortuga, as well as the Bahamas, the West Indies, Central America, and Mexico. The rare individual fish will be caught as far north as Massachusetts in midsummer. The permit is known as the Mexican pompano by many Gulf Coast anglers who find them as far north as Appalachicola, Panama City, and Pensacola, Florida; and as far west as Brownsville, Texas.

**Color**    The permit's body is a grayish silver-blue with a touch of yellow-orange on the belly. The fins are dark gray.

**Identifying characteristics**    The adult permit is oblong with a small mouth, blunt, high forehead and crescent-shaped tail. It is often confused with its relative, the common pompano. However, the permit can be positively identified by its shorter dorsal and anal fins, and the large second and third ribs, which can easily be felt through the skin. The permit is a much larger fish than other pompanos, often weighing as much as forty or fifty pounds.

**Size**    Permit average between ten and fifteen pounds, though twenty-five pounders are not uncommon. Many serious permit fishers believe sixty-pound fish exist and can be caught on a fly rod.

*Wandering the flats in search of permit can be time-consuming. Patience is required.*

The all-tackle world record is a fifty-pound, eight-ounce bruiser caught in Lake Worth, Florida. The fly-tackle world-record permit weighed in at forty-one pounds, eight ounces when caught on a 16-lb. test tippet at Key West, Florida, in 1986.

**Spawning period**

Most western Atlantic permit spawn in warm water during May and June about two hundred miles off the Florida coast.

**Angling notes**

The permit skittishly feeds around the edges of saltwater flats, nuzzling the sand for crustaceans and shrimp. This shy and nervous loner is extremely wary not only of humans, but also of all artificial lures and flies. The permit is a notoriously difficult fish to catch. It is regarded by professional anglers as more discriminating than bonefish and a much tougher fight, with twenty- and thirty-pound specimens often battling the flats angler over a half-mile of tidal water.

When hooked, the permit can go fifteen rounds with any brand of light tackle. It has a stocky, muscular body that makes it one of the toughest fighters of the saltwater flats. The permit's mouth is iron-tough; it requires sharp hooks and repeated strikes to set the hook. Then the fish will tear off two and three hundred-yard runs not once, but twice and three times, before the angler can begin to work it close. Permit will easily break off line and leader if too much rod leverage is

© Doug Perrine

*The shy permit feeds on crustaceans and shrimp in the sandy bottoms of saltwater reefs and flats. Permit are wary not only of human intruders in their environment, but also of any artificial lure or fly.*

*Medium saltwater spinning tackle is appropriate for most permit fishing. This Orvis saltwater spinning reel would serve an angler well on the shallow flats where long-distance casts are crucial.*

applied, often bumping their heads against the sea bottom in attempts to dislodge the hook. It is this combination of fighting qualities that makes the permit perhaps the ultimate prey for the saltwater fly fisherman.

Medium saltwater spinning tackle is the best match for the permit, either casting jigs or small pieces of the permit's favorite foods, crab and shrimp. This is perhaps one fish not to play too fine on light tackle; hookups are so rare, and the fish so strong that the odds against the angler are already very high. Permit often travel in schools, and in groups they are nearly impossible to catch, except when feeding near the surface on skeins of drifting shellfish and shrimp when their hunger makes them vulnerable to bait casting. Fly and spin fishers prefer casting to single or double permit as they feed on the flats. Permit hot spots around Florida, the Keys, and the Bahamas include Key West, Borroughs Cay, Boca Paila off Yucatan, Chub Cay in the Bahamas, and the unpopulated Keys. Fishing wrecks and reefs for permit is a higher percentage operation than flat fishing.

**Lures**  Bonefish jigs such as the Wiggle Jig, feather lures, small Rebel, Cotton Cordell or Rapala plugs, silvery spoons, and bucktail jigs are all worth a try but not likely to draw strikes. Most anglers feel that if they're going to fish artificial lures, they ought to use the fly rod, which offers similar odds but a more exciting fight and the highest cachet among their peers.

**Bait**  Crabs, crawfish, conch, hermit crab, or shrimp should be fished on the sandy bottom but never cast too close to the feeding permit, which spooks easily.

**Flies**  Dave's Salt Crab, White, Tan, and Pink Moes, Deceiver, and Marabou Charlie all work well. Many bonefish flies will double for permit, especially the shrimp and crab varieties. Crab imitations are especially effective.

**Best tackle**  Fly fishermen should use 9- to 9½-foot rods and 8- or 9-weight fly line. A strong saltwater fly reel with at least three hundred yards of backing is essential. The most popular permit rig involves a 6½ or seven-foot medium-action spinning rod, and a large-capacity saltwater spinning reel holding around 350 yards of 8- to 12-lb.-test monofilament. Some anglers prefer the low-gear ratios and antireverse drag of bait-casting tackle, which does require a great deal of skill in delivering baits of lures over long casting distances, but provides better fish-fighting leverage against the multiple long-distance touch-down runs of the permit.

# SAILFISH

*S*ome anglers are of the firm opinion that sailfish are more fun to go after than marlin, citing three reasons. First, sailfish are more numerous and therefore easier to find than marlin. Secondly, they are big enough to generate excitement as the best fish, but not so big that it takes hours to land them. Finally, sailfish have proved to be quite catchable on light tackle, including the fly rod.

—Michael Baughman, *Ocean Fishing*

SAILFISH (Pacific)

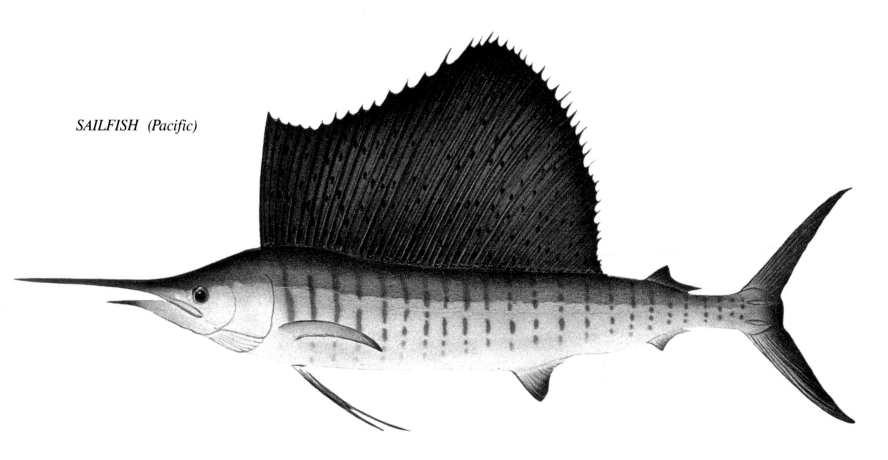

SAILFISH  *(Atlantic)*

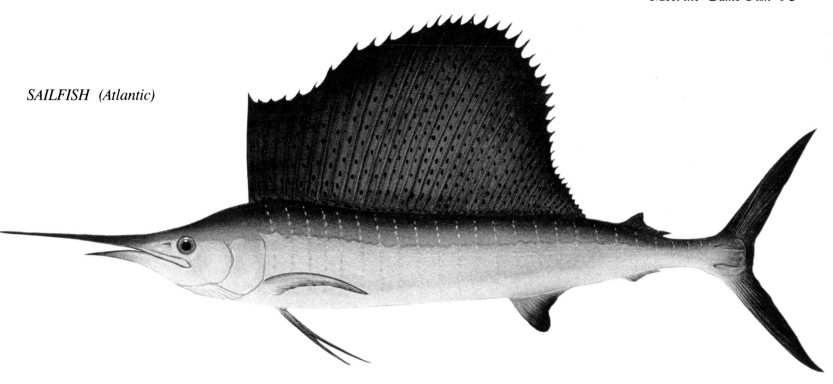

**Range**   Atlantic sailfish are found throughout the tropical Atlantic, ranging as far north as Massachusetts. Atlantic sailfish migrate on a regular basis, swimming northward from feeding grounds off the coast of Florida and the Keys, but rarely moving farther north than Cape Hatteras, North Carolina. Pacific sailfish are widely distributed throughout the tropical Pacific and Indian oceans. Mexican cities such as Acapulco, Mazatlan, and La Paz have become sailfishing meccas for veteran sport fishers and tourists the world over.

**Color**   The back of the sailfish is varying shades of metallic blue that blend into silvery sides and a white belly. The sail is cobalt blue and purple with vertical rows of small black dots.

**Identifying characteristics**   Anyone can mark a sailfish by the large saillike dorsal fin, which finds into a groove on the fish's back. The sail is extended when the fish is excited or comes to the surface.

**Size**   The Atlantic and Pacific sailfish are distinctly different in size, with the Pacific sails running about twice as big. Few sailfish landed in the Atlantic are smaller than twenty-five pounds or larger than fifty. Most Pacific sails fought on rod and reel average about a hundred pounds, with 120- and 130-pounders occurring regularly. The all-tackle world-record Atlantic sailfish was a 135-pound, 5-ounce fish caught near Lagos, Nigeria, in 1991. The world-record Pacific sail, weighing 221 pounds, was caught off the coast of Ecuador in 1947.

**Spawning period**   The Atlantic sail spawns between May and July in the flats around Florida and other coastal waters in the southern Atlantic and Caribbean.

© Tim Choate

*The sailfish is highly acrobatic once hooked.*

**Angling notes**

Sailfish are seasonally migratory billfish that are found in tropical and subtropical waters near land masses, usually in water over thirty feet deep. They will generally travel alone or in small groups, feeding in middle depths along the edges of reefs and current eddies. Fishing is best and most spectacular when sails chase schools of baitfish such as minnows to the surface where they surround them and drive them into a tightly packed group. They then slash through the baitfish in a highly profitable feeding session.

Acrobatic, eager, well distributed, and of managable size, the sailfish is a favorite pelagic gamefish. Sport-fishing captains take thousands of anglers out in the warm, open waters of the Pacific and Atlantic to catch this free-spirited acrobat. The sailfish is plentiful in both the Atlantic and Pacific, a challenging but hardly impossible adversary on light and even fly-fishing tackle. An exuberant, willful fighter capable of eight, nine or ten leaps in a typical half-hour battle, it can be handled on heavy saltwater fly tackle, light spinning tackle, and other variations. Few fish can surpass the excitement generated by a sailfish as it slashes across the open sea toward the trolling mullet or balao, approaches the prey from behind, taps the bait with its beak, and slams it with predatory fury.

Sailfishing hot spots in North

America include Cozumel off the Yucatan, the central Florida coast, and Cape Hatteras in summer.

**Lures**

More and more anglers with a sense of adventure are fighting sails with light spinning or fly tackle. Sure, some will be lost, but if you're not losing fish, you're not enjoying the most sporting excitement for your sailfishing money and effort—and usually where there's one sail, more will follow. To bring the angler's light tackle into play, the captain will often troll a hookless bait or bright attractor directly behind the boat to attract the curious or hungry sail; when the fish is within casting distance, the angler swings his or her rod into action, delivering a spoon, plug, or streamer to the snapping, frothed-up sailfish. Having reached this stage of excitement, the sailfish will almost always hit the lure, and when it does, the angler will hook into one of the supreme light-tackle challenges of life. Any sail caught on 20-lb. test provides scintillating action and requires a good deal of skill to land. Slow trolling of plastic squid like the Chummin' Squid or Squirt Squid is an extremely reliable technique for taking sailfish; of course, the trolling lures like the Konahead or Tournament Tackle Illander in small sizes are frequently used and very reliable.

**Bait**

Mullet, balao, sand perch, grunts, or herring trolled at high speed for skipping action, if dead, or trolled around five or six knots if alive.

**Flies**

Very large, silvery streamers are the ticket.

**Best tackle**

If drawn close to the boat, sailfish can be taken on big saltwater fly rods and streamers with ten- or twelve-weight fly line, 16- or 18 lb.-test tippet, and about 250 yards of backing on a sturdy fly reel. Light 20- and 30-lb. boat tackle strung with 20-lb. test is all the trolling angler needs in the Atlantic, while Pacific anglers chasing the largest sails might need to up the tackle weight class by about a third. Leaders generally are composed of two feet of six- to eight-weight wire and twelve feet of 60- to 80-lb.-test monofilament and 4/0 to 6/0 hooks.

*Trolling is the most generally effective method of successful sailfishing, though once attracted by the trolling lure, sails can be plied with plugs or even flies.*

# COHO AND CHINOOK SALMON

*O to break loose, like the chinook*

*salmon jumping and falling back,*

*nosing up the impossible*

*stone and bone-crushing waterfall—*

*raw-jawed, weak-fleshed there,*

*stopped by ten steps of the roaring ladder, and then to*

*clear the top on the last try,*

*alive enough to spawn and die.*

—Robert Lowell, *Walking Early Sunday Morning*

COHO

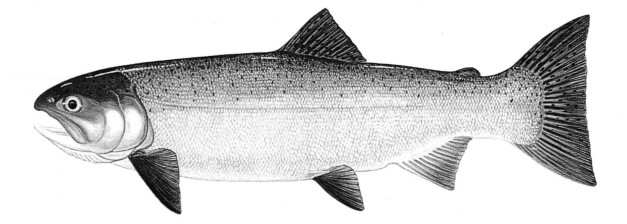

*CHINOOK (Female)*

While both of these Pacific species are pursued extensively by sport fishermen in salt water, significant freshwater angling takes place in the Pacific freshwater estuaries and rivers where the coho and chinook return to spawn and most impressively in the Great Lakes, where the stocking of coho salmon has seen enormous success.

**Range**

Cohos and chinooks range throughout the Pacific Coast, from Oregon and Washington to northern California. They now thrive in the Great Lakes. On the Pacific, coho and chinook return to the freshwater rivers of their birth to spawn, and in the Great Lakes, the first-generation spawning salmon will initiate the freshwater rivers that will then become the permanent spawning grounds for their progeny.

**Color**

The coho has a blue-black back that fades to silver flanks and white belly. Black spots appear on the back and upper part of the coho salmon's tail.

The chinook is generally a more muscular, broader fish than the coho. The chinook also has a wider distribution of black spots and a darker colored back.

**Identifying characteristics**

The coho's mouth is usually gray or black with whitish gums. The chinook's jaws feature a full set of small teeth; the coho shows only a few.

**Spawning period**

Coho spawn in the rivers where they were born during late fall and winter, entering freshwater in late summer. After birth, young coho spend about a year in freshwater and then migrate to the sea, reaching adulthood at three or four years of age, when they turn for home in the arduous struggle to reproduce. The chinook spawns in the large freshwater rivers of the Northwest from June to November. Spawning cycles are complicated, occurring in some rivers every month of the year when each run of salmon heads for one particular tributary or portion of the river's headwaters. Chinook fry take varying amounts of time to mature and migrate to sea where they will forage vast stretches of ocean, growing at a rate of three to six pounds a year. After about five years of growth, the adults return to spawn, often traveling extraordinary distances. Tagged Pacific salmon have been known

© Dan Polin

*This angler has hooked a big chinook in Hakai Pass, British Columbia. When landed, the salmon would tip the scales at 40 pounds.*

to travel up to 2,750 miles at an average speed of forty miles a day. After spawning, all Pacific salmon die.

The salmon's heroic upriver struggle against natural and man-made obstacles and predators has inspired many articles, books, and poems. Every aspect of the salmon run is tinged with the nobility of unvanquished determination against nearly insurmountable odds. This passage from Roger Carras's *Sockeye* illustrates the point:

And the mathematics of it? How do salmon numbers fare? [A spawning adult] is one of just 3600 fertile eggs that had been placed in the gravel by his mother and father .... Of the 3600, 106 smolt had made it through the lake and as far as the sea. Of those 106, ten survived to reach the mouth of the Coppertree System again. But there was the final test, for of those ten, eight would die in their

attempts to move upstream. Two of the more than 3600 eggs . . . would reach their natal bed and spawn.

In the Great Lakes, both coho and chinook follow fall spawning migration patterns, entering the rivers of Michigan, Illinois, and New York in October and November. Mature fish caught early in the spawning cycle are top angling prizes. Spinning and plug casting for spawning-run cohos in river inlets and shallows offer some of the most exciting and accessible sporting challenges in America.

**Angling notes**

Pacific coast: The majority of coho and chinook fishing is done at sea from charter and private boats with herring downriggers. Deeper into the year, the salmon feed closer to the surface, and diving plane herring or anchovy rigs, crankbaits, and large, brightly colored spoons are all very effective. Once the salmon are found, they can most definitely be caught. When coho are feeding near the surface, enterprising anglers

*Wherever the Pacific salmon heads home to reproduce, anglers will congregate. These trolling boats crowd the harbor in Sitka, Alaska, premium salmon country where fishing is the main means of economic support.*

*Long rods and baitcasting reels are the tools required when drift-fishing, mooching, or bait-fishing for salmon.*

*Two hefty chinooks that will make delectable salmon steaks.*

© Francis & Donna Caldwell

will tempt them with a streamer and fight the fish on a large fly rod—or work the moiling topwater with plugs and spoons on light spinning gear. As you might guess, fighting a ten-pound coho on light spinning tackle more than fulfills the angler's minimum daily hard work requirements. After coho and chinook enter the great rivers of the Northwest—leading salmon freshwater includes the Columbia, Willamette, Skeena, Campbell, Sacramento, and Fraser Rivers—a variety of angling methods may be employed to catch the homing salmon during their short days of travel to the spawning grounds, depending on local catch regulations. Drifting eggs or shrimp on Spin-N-Glo drift bobbers, mooching (or slow trolling), wet fly fishing, and deep spinning are all popular methods.

**Best tackle** For trolling, use 20- to 30-lb. test on a medium heavy trolling reel, a 6.5- to seven-foot 2/0-3/0 fiberglass rod, and terminal tackle that incorporates a 30-lb. or so mono leader, flashers or dodgers to attract the salmon, snelled hooks, and bait. For fly fishing, nine- or ten-foot rods are essential, and for larger chinooks, rods can go as long as twelve feet. Use sinking weight forward fly line, a short leader, and big hooks for chinook; try smaller ones for coho.

© Ruth Fairall

**Trolling for salmon in Prince William Sound, Alaska, site of the 1989 oil spill.**

# SHARKS

*H*is back was as blue as a swordfish's, and his belly was silver and his hide was smooth and handsome. He was built as a swordfish except for his huge jaws which were tight shut now as he swam fast, just under the surface with his high dorsal fin knifing through the water without wavering. Inside the closed double lip of his jaws all of his eight rows of teeth were slanted inwards. They were not the ordinary pyramid-shaped teeth of most sharks. They were shaped like a man's fingers when they are crisped like claws. They were nearly as long as the fingers of the old man and they had razor-sharp cutting edges on both sides. This was a fish built to feed on all the fishes in the sea that were so fast and strong and well armed that they had no other enemy. Now he speeded up as he smelled the fresher scent and his blue dorsal fin cut the water.

—Ernest Hemingway, *The Old Man and The Sea*

TIGER SHARK

© Philip Rosenberg

***Evolution's most perfectly-designed killing machine.***

The world's most relentless predatory machine (except, perhaps, for the bluefish) and the once and future sovereign of the oceanic food chain, the shark with its deservedly fierce reputation is now the favorite meal of the supreme predator of the oceans, the sport boat. The middle class has adopted big-game fishing as a weekend activity on par with beach-going and barbequeing, and the shark has emerged as a favorite target, especially in northeastern waters. Its fearsome meat-eating style spurs the urge of the great North American gamefisher to prove his or her mettle before this simple creature of the deep that lacks the power of reason but would look darn impressive on a basement wall. The shark makes itself widely available to the sport-boat denizens with its omnivorous appetite that shows little discrimination for artificially rigged bait. The result is a booming shark sport-fishery featuring many tournaments and contests, and bringing to the dock thousands of trussed blues and makos, ready to be sawed up and filleted for Sunday's barbeque, their heavy-tackle submission exaggerated in tales of Spielbergian derring-do.

**Range** The common blue shark is the most numerous of popular "game" sharks found in North America, which include makos, tigers, whites, and hammerheads. Sport fishermen will also fish for porbeagle, bull, blacktip, and dusky sharks, but the species discussed here are runaway favorites for their size, ferocity, and availability.

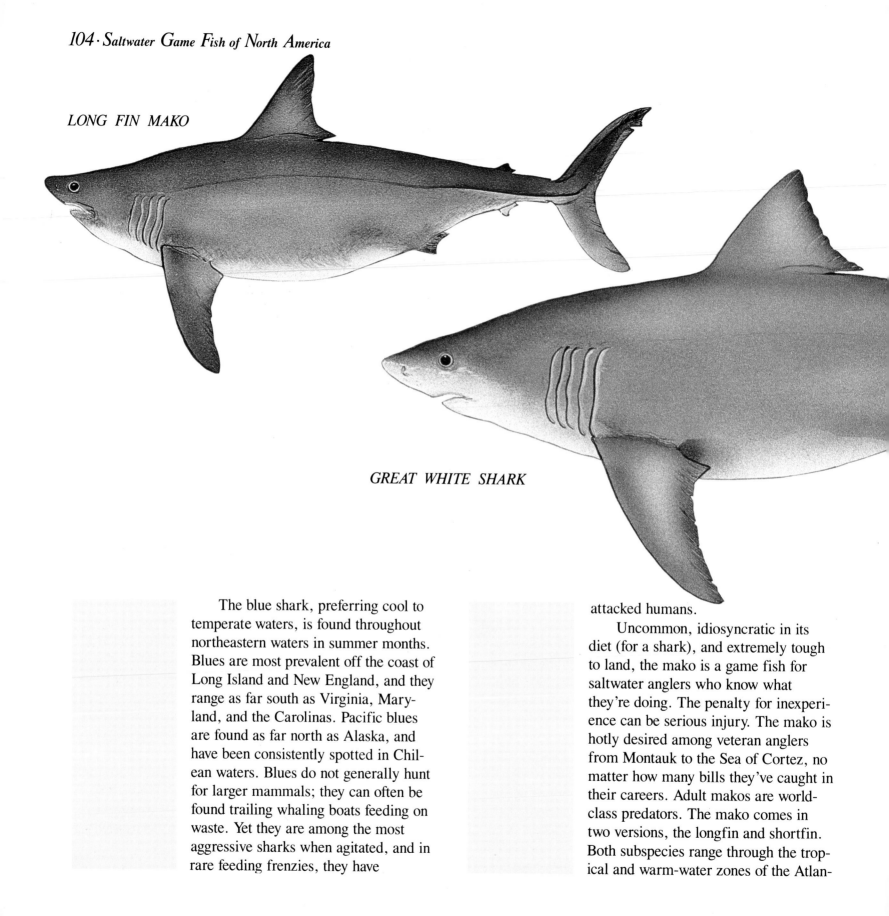

*LONG FIN MAKO*

*GREAT WHITE SHARK*

The blue shark, preferring cool to temperate waters, is found throughout northeastern waters in summer months. Blues are most prevalent off the coast of Long Island and New England, and they range as far south as Virginia, Maryland, and the Carolinas. Pacific blues are found as far north as Alaska, and have been consistently spotted in Chilean waters. Blues do not generally hunt for larger mammals; they can often be found trailing whaling boats feeding on waste. Yet they are among the most aggressive sharks when agitated, and in rare feeding frenzies, they have attacked humans.

Uncommon, idiosyncratic in its diet (for a shark), and extremely tough to land, the mako is a game fish for saltwater anglers who know what they're doing. The penalty for inexperience can be serious injury. The mako is hotly desired among veteran anglers from Montauk to the Sea of Cortez, no matter how many bills they've caught in their careers. Adult makos are world-class predators. The mako comes in two versions, the longfin and shortfin. Both subspecies range through the tropical and warm-water zones of the Atlan-

BLUE SHARK

SMOOTH HAMMERHEAD SHARK

tic and Pacific. The shortfin, however, will often hunt inshore, which makes it the far more common prey of boat captains. It also seems, from available evidence, to be the more widely distributed mako, occurring in the Atlantic from Cape Cod to Argentina, including the Gulf of Mexico and the Caribbean, and in the Pacific from the Columbia River in summer to California coastal waters and as far south as Chile year-round.

Mako have been spotted in the Gulf of California. The longfin mako is a rarer species that favors the open seas of the Caribbean and Pacific. Few longfin mako have ever been caught off the Atlantic coast or Gulf of Mexico. The mako ranks among the most dangerous of sharks, and knowledgeable sport fishermen approach them with great care. They are cauldrons of fury when hooked. Although their twenty- and thirty-foot aerial jumps are exciting, makos will often try to ram or even leap into the "enemy's" boat. No shark should be brought boat-side or onto the deck until it is completely exhausted—a "green" shark brought close to overconfident anglers can cause serious injury.

**Great White Shark**

A wounded mako, like most other sharks, can bite with strength until drawing its very last breath.

Tiger sharks prowl the inshore and open waters of the southern Atlantic, Gulf of Mexico, West Indies, and Caribbean, and frequent warm Pacific waters from southern California to Peru. They are occasionally found off the Northeast and Pacific Northwest coasts in summer. Tigers are tireless, omnivorous feeders that attack everything, anytime, anywhere. They are tenacious, acrobatic, and terribly strong when hooked, and they provide even seasoned big-game bounty hunters a full test of skill. The result is a shark very popular with big-game fishing captains around the world.

The tiger sharks' eating habits make it a good bet for the trophy room, but its aggressive tendencies in shallow water have never been good news for recreationists. Tigers are omnivorous predators that pose the greatest danger of all sharks to human beings, prowling the shore waters where people swim and boat, possessed of a relentless drive to attack and eat any easily available prey. Tigers have attacked scores of swimmers off the coasts of Florida and Australia—though it must be remembered that the percentage of those attacked is so small in relation to the millions of total swimmers on North American beaches that a shark attack could be compared in probability to being struck by lightning. Tiger sharks will eat anything, as people cutting open their stomachs have found. The tiger is the source of the shark's reputation for omnivorousness, and its diet has included fish, crabs, turtles, stingrays, birds, other sharks, nuts and bolts, lumps of coal, articles of clothing, boat cushions, tin cans, various garbage, human limbs, the hind leg of a sheep, and even a coil of copper wire.

Tiger shark hunters must treat this eating machine with utmost care. Tigers will sometimes try to ram or jump into a boat, often before they are hooked, to reach the source of the chum that drew them to the boat. When hooked, they should be fought until they are rolling on their backs with exhaustion; the kill should be made before bringing them on deck.

The white shark inspires in humans the greatest fears of the deep and the man-eating sea monsters that inhabit it. The great white's fearsomeness centers not only on its reputation for attacking human beings, but also in the sheer size of its predatory parts—the jaws, the teeth, the head—that make it very clear how small a person's odds would be if the shark forced a confrontation. Like the demon octopi and whales of legend, the white has a reputation for destroying ships unprovoked, and then eating the contents.

Humans seem to need these symbols to give shape, form, and relief to our fears of the sea and its drowning depths. *Jaws* and its ilk have disseminated a myth of malevolent intelligence about the white that adds to its primal terror. Nevertheless, many sport fishers have overcome their fear and fish for the white as sport. Or perhaps they have not overcome their fear after all . . .

The white grows to weights of over a ton, which makes it the ocean's largest predator save for the killer whales. It prefers cooler waters, and its range is among the widest of all sharks. Whites have been recorded as far north as Alaska and throughout Pacific coast waters, preferring the cooler inshore currents that can bring them quite close to land (and seals, which are a favorite meal). Whites have attacked numerous swimmers and divers in these coastal streams, especially near San Francisco. Again, the odds of attack are slim, but they will be even slimmer if boaters and swimmers check on shark conditions with lifeguards, fishing officials, or the Coast Guard before swimming or playing in open water. Spotted as far north as Nova Scotia on the Atlantic coast, the white frequents southern waters around Florida, the Gulf of Mexico, and the West Indies, and ranges as far south as Brazil. Many whites have been spotted off the Northeast shores, particularly around Long Island during the summer. In 1916, a great white attacked and killed two people in Matawan Creek, New Jersey, the last great white attack in Northeastern shore waters. They are common, too, off the Australian and New Zealand northern coasts, where they have often been filmed battering the shark cages of squirming professional divers and photographers.

The shark's brain is very large for its size, comparable in proportion to body weight with mammals, and it is equipped with huge sensory centers. The shark has developed with electroreceptors that can detect very low-frequency sounds, acting as a sort of geomagnetic compass to orient the shark to sources of struggle, disturbed motion, and other movements that indicate wounded prey, schools of fish, and geographical features. The shark's fore-

*Played sharks must be handled extremely carefully during landing and gaffing. A shark is not ready to be brought aboard until it is rolling with exhaustion, and if it is of any size and you wish to keep it, it should first be killed.*

© Marty Snyderman

brain is almost entirely comprised of olfactory lobes, which are extremely sensitive to a range of amino acids and amines associated with live, wounded, or dead prey. The midbrain, largely used for vision, holds two optic lobes. The hindbrain, which is the shark's cerebellum, coordinates its motion and other senses.

Yet a shark's behavior can make one wonder about its intelligence. It is clear that the brain evolved in the service of one function: To find and kill prey in the open seas. Attacked and multilated sharks have repeatedly been seen feeding on their own viscera, and injured sharks will continue feeding or attacking until they can no longer move.

**Color**

The blue shark is aptly named and easily identified. Its back is dark blue, its flanks tinted a brighter and more silvery blue, and its belly is white. Makos are also brilliantly colored, cobalt blue-gray or darker blue on back, brightening to light blue on the flanks and white below. The lower jaw is white.

Young tiger sharks are banded with dark brown vertical stripes from gill slits to tail and dark brown spots are sprayed across the back. As tiger sharks mature, these juvenile markings fade to brownish gray or ochre. The tiger's belly varies between white and white-gray. Faint stripes and spots can occasionally be seen on the adult tiger.

The white shark is white only on its belly. Its submarine-sized body will vary from dark to light brown-gray. Its pectoral fins are tipped with black.

**Identifying characteristics**

The most precise method of identifying sharks is by comparing their teeth; however, this is not very practical for the angler who may not want to open the shark's jaws and start examining serrations and bite angles until the potential trophy is well into rigor mortis. And there are many anglers who don't want to keep a shark unless it is a particularly large prize of a particular species. So there are other methods.

The blue shark, with its electric-blue coloration, very slender spindle shape, and long, pointed doggish snout is among the easiest sharks to identify on the spot. The tips of its fins are edged in gray, the pectorals are long and narrow. Its teeth are shaped like sabers, one margin concave, and the other convex. The blue's dorsal fins are smaller and less dramatic than those of the mako, white, or tiger.

The great white and mako are both mackerel sharks (torpedo-shaped bodies, large teeth), and the great white can be distinguished by the full-bodied chest and narrowing lower back and tail that form a streamlined torpedo shape. The snouts of the white and mako are conical, ending in a point. There are large, prominent flattened keels on either side of the caudal peduncle. On both the great white and the mako, the first dorsal fin is much larger than the second. The mako's teeth are relatively few, slender and smooth edged, in contrast to the serrated, triangular teeth of the white.

The easiest way for the oceangoing angler to distinguish the white from the mako, which are similarly shaped and sized, is through the mako's bright blue back. Mako are also torpedo-shaped, and they feature the legendary large dorsal fin. Their caudal peduncle keels are flattened as are those of the white shark. The longfin mako has a blunter snout and larger eye than the shortfin. Its pectoral fins are much larger.

The tiger shark is among the largest sharks, and can be confused with the white because of its coloration. The tiger's first dorsal fin is again much larger than the second. The tiger's snout is clearly blunter and rounder than the white's or mako's, and the tiger's teeth are exceptionally easy to identify because they are notched and broad at the bottom with sharp serrations. The bodies of smaller juvenile tigers are marked with stripes or bars. The gill slits of the mako and white do not extend beyond the pectoral fin, but the tiger's last two or three gill slits are positioned well beyond and above the pectoral fin.

NOTE: Never attempt to examine a shark's teeth until three or four hours after its death.

**Size**

When young, blue sharks are such willing feeders that they can be caught virtually every time the bait gets near them, which makes blues popular with high-yield shark-fishing boats. Often the same blue shark will be caught two or three times in the same day. Immature blues run from thirty to a hundred pounds; the adult blues, which still comprise the majority catch of the six-pack day fleets after shark, weigh between 200 and 350 pounds.

Adult makos reach weights of four and five hundred pounds and up. The all-tackle world record is a 1,080-pound mako caught off Block Island on August 26, 1979 by Captain Frank Mundus, the legendary shark angler, who was the inspiration for Peter Benchley's shark hunter in *Jaws*. Anglers in search of mako catch relatively few large specimens, and any fish of 350 pounds or more is considered a handsome win.

Among the largest creatures of the sea and the largest of the sharks (except for the great white), tigers have been caught consistently on rod and reel at weights of over one thousand pounds; the all-tackle world record is a 1,780-pound shark caught off the shores of South Carolina in 1964.

In a network-televised, anything-goes battle to the death between the great white and the killer shark, the odds would be close to even. These two magnificent murderers have no competition that swims without the help of a motor. The great white, for example, has demonstrated a casual willingness to feed on humans regardless of their occupations, real estate holdings, country club memberships or political affiliations. The adult great white matures to between six hundred and a thousand pounds, though regional influences, diet, and range have their effect on size. Older great whites, of course, grow much larger. A number of two thousand-pound fish have been caught and the largest fish ever taken on a rod and reel was a 3,427-pound great white caught off Montauk, Long Island, by Captains Frank Mundus and Donnie Braddick. That fish weighed more than a pickup truck carrying a medium-sized boat, more than the entire starting defense of the New York Giants, and more than a half-dozen American buffalo.

**Spawning period**

Sharks are classified by their spawning habits with these three terms: viviparous (bearing live young), oviparous (producing eggs that hatch outside the body), and ovoviviparous (an evolutionary way station between bearing eggs and bearing young found in some sharks, who hatch young from eggs within the womb where they grow for a few days before being born into the water, swimming freely).

The blue shark is viviparous; it gives birth to fifty or more live young. Blues reach maturity at about the length of seven feet. The tiger shark is also viviparous. Both the mako and white shark are ovoviviparous.

*The leaping Mako is the most prized shark among veteran big-game anglers.*

**Angling notes** The shark dominates the seas because it does one thing very well: It attacks food and eats it. Ironically, the shark is the easiest of the big-game catches because it can't stop eating. Shark do not discriminate or vacillate. Wherever food is available, they will get there first, attack first, and eat the fastest. For the angler or shark captain this means using bait, either live or filleted, on large hooks with steel leaders.

Even white and tiger shark fishers need go no larger than size 6/0 boat tackle, and for virtually all shark fishing situations, 3/0 to 4/0 class tackle rigged with 30- to 50-lb.-test line, number 12 wire leaders and 9/0 hooks provides all the necessary power to fight sharks in the 250 to 750-pound class. More than ninety percent of shark catches fall in that range.

The waters of Montauk on Long Island offer the most consistent shark fishing north of the Caribbean, and the possibility for catching a genuine sea monster there does exist. Numerous shark tournaments are organized out of Montauk during the summer. The Bahamas and Florida Keys are also leading centers of shark-fishing activity; few are the days in those waters when a charter captain after shark will return empty-handed. Blue shark fishing in southern California waters (off Point Conception) is highly popular. Here fishing boats will often take hundreds of blues in a single day. Hammerhead fishing in the Sea of Cortez is booming and popular among California sportsmen. In short, there is plenty of satisfaction available for those who want to bust the baddest fish of the seas.

# SNOOK
## (Robalo, Saltwater Pike)

*SNOOK*

**Range**  Snook range through the western tropical Atlantic, from Florida to Brazil, including the Gulf of Mexico; they are also found in the eastern tropical Pacific from Baja to Peru. The snook is commonly found inshore, often in brackish water. Favorite habitats are near bridges and docks; in lagoons, canals, streams, and estuaries; and occasionally the upper reaches of tidal rivers. Snook need warm water, and they will stop feeding as water temperature falls below sixty degrees; this limits their North American distribution to southern Florida on the Atlantic and Gulf sides. The largest snook are caught in bays and inlets along the east coast from Vero Beach to Miami, and on the Gulf side from Boca Grande south to the Everglades.

**Color**  The snook's back may be brown, brown-gold, blue-green, dark gray, olive, or black depending on the season, habitat, and other conditions. The belly is silvery.

**Identifying characteristics**  The snook is easily recognizable. It has a protruding lower jaw and a highly prominent black lateral line that runs from the top of the gill, along the sides, and all the way to the tail. The gill covers have sharp serrated edges.

**Size**  The average snook weighs in at around eighteen to twenty-three pounds.

**Spawning period**

Snook spawn in summer when water temperatures are warmest.

**Angling notes**

The snook's favorite foods are fish and crustaceans. Trolling or casting artificial lures is quite successful, as is still fishing with live bait such as pinfish, mullet, shrimp, or crab. Try fishing for snook in freshwater-saltwater meeting points when the tide is changing. High ebb tide in brackish tidal rivers and delta waters is especially auspicious. Snook will hit top-water plugs among the mangroves and structures of tidal rivers and estuaries with the ferocity of the gamest largemouth. Night casting from bridges and in ocean inlets can lead to hot snook fishing.

**Best tackle**

Snook should generally be fished as if they were big largemouth bass, with heavy freshwater or light saltwater bait-casting tackle (or spinning if long, accurate casts are called for), plugs, and a wire leader to protect against their razor-sharp gill covers.

© Doug Perrine

*Like largemouth bass, snook prefer to hold in the structure of reefs, rocks, mangrove roots, or other formations, and wait until something appealing for dinner swims by. Anglers should therefore cast their lures close to likely holds, and be resigned to losing a few plugs in snags.*

# SWORDFISH

## (Broadbill)

*S*wordfishing takes more time, patience, endurance, skill, nerve and strength, not to mention money, than any game known to me through experience or reading.

—Zane Grey, *Tales of Swordfish and Tuna*

*BROADBILL SWORDFISH*

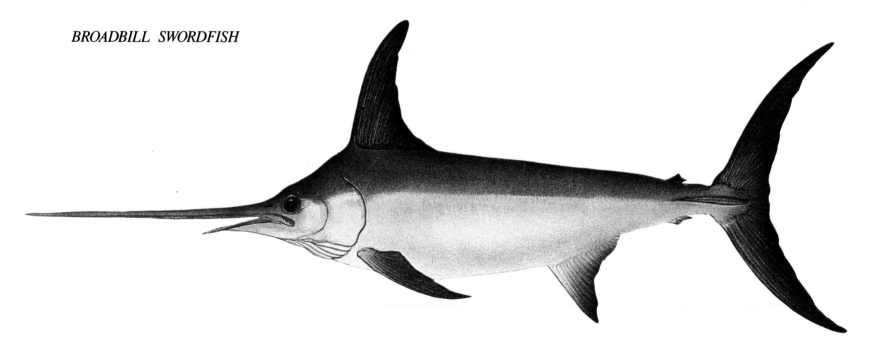

**Range**    Widespread throughout the tropical seas of the world, the swordfish will travel far north in summer, appearing regularly off the northeast coasts of Canada and the United States, and in the waters of northern California.

Swordfish travel alone or in pods of three or four widely separated fish.

They will feed at any depth, and bottom-dwelling fish found at depths of one thousand feet have been discovered in swordfish stomachs. Swordfish are often seen, especially at night, resting on the surface with their tall dorsal fin protruding from the water. The broadbill will not strike at bait in this repose.

Ichthyologists believe swordfish can attain swimming speeds of sixty mph, with the sword acting as a hydrofoil to break the water in front of them. The bill is also believed by some to be a weapon to stun and kill squid and favorite finned prey, including mackerel, jacks, bluefish, dolphin and numerous other mid- and deep-water species.

The sievelike gills of the swordfish allow it to process a great deal of oxygen, which maintains its high circulatory rate and body temperature for high-speed swimming and striking. When hooked, the swordfish is one of the ocean's most unforgiving adversaries—acrobatic, ferociously strong, and capable of high leaps and sounding dives to the bottom of the ocean.

There are stories about swordfish attacking boats, and many of them are true. For example, one swordfish attacked Alvin, the submersible boat of the Woods Hole Oceanographic Institute, at a depth of 330 fathoms. The swordfish wedged its sword so tightly into a seam in the hull that it could not withdraw it. The broadbill has a porous ethmoid bone in the forepart of the skull that acts as a shock absorber when it uses its sword.

Naturalist E.W. Grudger uncovered this story of a Boston whaler: "When she reached harbour at Plymouth, Massachusetts in 1826 she had the sword of a swordfish in her hull that had penetrated a copper sheathing, 4 inches of board, solid oak a foot thick, 2.5 inches of hard oak ceiling plank and the head of an oil cask."

*A remarkable sight: a hatchling swordfish.*

**Color**  This beautifully streamlined predator has a high front dorsal fin that is short at the base and curves backwards. There are no pelvic fins. The first anal fin is large while the second and third anal fins are very small and set far back. The body is flattened on the sides, with dark purple-blue on the back shading to silvery gray on the underside. The sword is black above and pale gray below. Fins are dark and purplish with a silvery glaze.

**Identifying characteristics**  The long, flat sword is obviously unmistakable.

**Swordfishing is the supreme challenge for practitioners of open-water trolling.**

**Size**

Perhaps the most prized and respected game fish of the oceans, the swordfish can reach 1,200 pounds and more; adults commonly grow as large as six and seven hundred pounds. Most angling professionals and ichthyologists believe that older swordfish can grow much larger than the existing world record of 1,100 pounds, but they are so elusive, deep running, cautious, and nocturnal that catching them borders on the impossible.

**Spawning period**

Swordfish spawn in the open sea, in water of eighty-five degrees or more, from February to April in the tropical Atlantic and from June to August in the Mediterranean. The hatchlings drop deep into the sea to feed on plankton and other fish larvae.

**Angling notes**

Only professionals need apply. Angling for swordfish is the supreme challenge for practitioners of open-water trolling. Active saltwater anglers make a lucky catch once every few years, but only the most experienced anglers and professional captains catch swordfish by design. Swordfish are highly sensitive and are frightened by boats; they take their time in making a strike. They like to feed at night, and they like to feed deep. Their mouths are soft and difficult to hook; their slashing bill can cut even a wire line or leader. Zane Grey, perhaps the greatest big-game angler who ever lived, caught only six swordfish in a lifetime of fishing. During one period of fishing off Santa Catalina, Grey spotted no less than eighty-seven swordfish in ninety days. He trolled bait past seventy-five of them; of those, only a dozen were hooked and fought. Of those dozen, only one fish, a 418-pounder, was landed.

The most popular fishing method is to sight a resting swordfish on the surface—when it is positively off the feed—and slowly, from a great distance, drag a rigged baitfish across its nose. Sometimes this will arouse the sleeping broadbill, and it will slash at the bait in a sudden fit of territorial anger. If the swordfish hits the bait, the bait must be released and the fish allowed to "hold" the bait for at least ten seconds before setting the drag and striking.

Once hooked, the swordfish gives the angler unequalled battle. It will sound deep, and working it back to the surface can take hours. If the angler is lucky, the swordfish will begin its fight on top with spectacular displays of leaping and tail walking that tire the fish quickly. If the broadbill sounds on the strike and heads deep, however, the angler can expect a fight that can last a good part of the day or more. Most swordfish hookups begin fights that last for hours.

**Best tackle**

Trolling tackle of the 5/0 to 6/0 class is the minimum weaponry for swordfishing. They are too rare, too difficult to catch, and too hard to land to take any chances, and I mean any, with light tackle. Most captains going out for swords will take the heavy artillery of at least 7/0 boat tackle, and many will go to 100-lb. test and up.

Catching swordfish is a lifetime ambition. It is not for the faint of will or heart. Truthfully, it is supremely hard work. To the great black torpedo fish and those who choose to pursue it, best of luck.

# TARPON

## (Silver King)

*T*hat first time a 125-pound silver rocket goes off twenty feet from your skiff, gills jangling, water flying, you'll know what brought you to tarpon fishing. There is nothing like it—a big-game fish in a small-tackle environment. And every time it happens thereafter, it will take your breath away.

—Ted Williams, *Fishing the Big Three*

*TARPON*

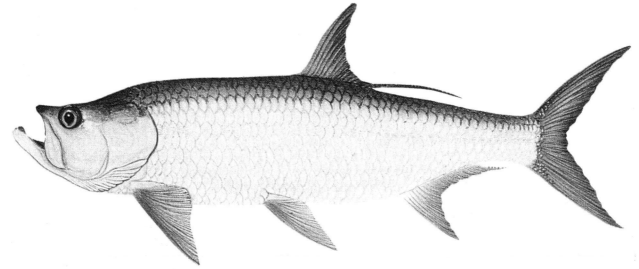

**Range** Tarpon are found as far south as Costa Rica and French Guiana and northward along the southern Atlantic coast; they are rife in the Gulf of Mexico and the Florida Keys where they inhabit estuaries, creeks, canals, saltwater and eelgrass flats, and other inland saltwater configurations. The larger fish roam the outer tidal channels and open waters of the Gulf of Mexico and southern Atlantic. Tarpon appear off the coasts of Texas, Louisiana, Georgia, and other southern states.

**Color** The tarpon is built like a giant herring, with a deep, compressed body that is

*Tarpon schooling near a coral reef. Larger tarpon are on the decline, their numbers reduced through over-fishing and devastation of coastal spawning areas.*

greenish blue on the back and sides, sloping to a silvery belly.

**Identifying characteristics**

The tarpon's lower jaw hinges out and up, fitting like a scoop over the upper jaw. The tarpon's body is covered with layered armorlike scales one to three inches in diameter, and the throat is protected by a similarly constructed bony plate. The dorsal fin is distinctively elongated.

**Size**

The silver king will average eighty-five to one hundred and fifteen pounds, while catches of forty- to sixty-pound fish are much more common in shallow water. The catching on rod and reel of any tarpon over two hundred pounds is an event. The world record was a monstrous 283-pound Venezuelan tarpon battled to its death in 1956.

**Spawning period**

The tarpon is one of the least understood game fish alive. Scientists and ichthyologists know little about their spawning and migrating habits, though they agree that tarpon spawn in open water. Tarpon fry drift inshore where they remain as juveniles until they reach about two feet in length. The building, dredging, filling, and pollution of hundreds of miles of Florida and Gulf Coast shoreline have destroyed many tarpon nursery areas and have therefore cut into schools of adult tarpon found on the Gulf Coast and elsewhere. Tarpon display heavy migratory activity in the spring; May and June in the Florida Keys are prime time for tarpon as they migrate north up the Gulf and Atlantic coasts from the Southern Atlantic.

**Angling notes**

This prehistoric piscine relic has

*No fish busts up light tackle like these—only a fraction of tarpon caught on rod and reel are landed.*

become one of saltwater fishing's most sought after prizes. For fight per pound, no saltwater fish beats the tarpon. End of story.

Only a fraction of the tarpon hooked on rod and reel are landed, for no fish, whether born in freshwater or brackish water, can match the tarpon's tackle-busting power. Not only does the fish leap so swiftly and high—often hurling itself ten feet above the water—that it can throw the hook before the angler can strike, but its mouth is also plated with tough armor-like jaws that

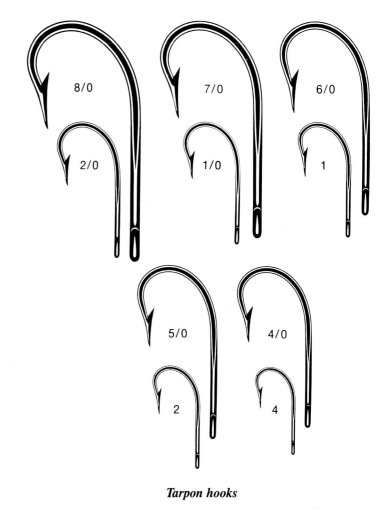

**Tarpon hooks**

resist penetration of the sharpest hooks.

Once this silver destroyer is hooked, however, the angler's challenge has just begun. The tarpon will throw itself in the air four, five, six, or more times, often either spitting the hook or snapping the line to break free, and if still on line, it will sound off on a reel-scorching, rail-rattling run across the flats like a freight train barreling full steam downhill. Then, if the trembling angler can exhaust the tarpon and eventually haul it boatside, the fish may still explode in a last series of desperate jumps which may even put it into the boat. If this happens, clear out into the water, and let the tarpon smash up the boat and tackle. It beats what it might do to you!

Local guides are usually mandatory in tarpon expeditions. Tarpon movements differ from one saltwater environment to the next, but they are generally found around the canals and tidal channels that bridge flats, estuaries, and inshore waters to the open ocean. Tarpon also wander these shallower waters on ebb and flow tides;

excellent fishing is often found in brackish rivers and at tidal choke points around islands, keys, and other land masses. The entire length of the Florida Keys produces reliable tarpon fishing from April to October. Most tarpon anglers use Islamorada as a base for the Upper Keys, Marathon for the Middle Keys, and Key West for the Southern Keys and Marquesas. Tarpon Springs and Homosassa Springs on the Gulf Coast provide more experienced tarpon fishers with schools of larger, less willing specimens to ply with the newest flies and lures every spring.

Captains favor trolling rods and reels with their usually inexperienced customers, for heavier tackle offers better probability of boating a fish. Veterans of the flats prefer spinning or bait-casting gear, depending on the size of the tarpon they expect to encounter. Casting to sighted fish is the most satisfying form of tarpon angling. Many fly fishermen will claim that hooking and landing a tarpon on heavy fly-fishing tackle is the most thrilling event in the sport. Bonefish may be more elusive, but the tarpon makes for a faster heartbeat and sweatier palms. Adult tarpon are nocturnal, and night fishing can produce spectacularly large fish.

**Lures**

Tarpon will usually hit large, silver mullet plugs like the Arbogast Scudder, needlefish imitations, yellow, brown, white, and silver large jigs like the Gaines Poxy Flies and Poppers, and bucktail streamers.

**Bait**

A tarpon will take any number of live and dead bait, including crabs, mullet, shrimp, catfish, pinfish, and needle-fish. Bait is either drifted to sighted schools of tarpon with a float or "balloon" to suspend it in midwater, or slowly trolled with a stainless steel leader.

**Flies**

Use large streamers and popping and darting bugs, such as the Orange Grizzly, Tarpon Cockroach, Blue Death Tarpon, Blue Death, Pink Fluff, Chinese Claw, Stu Apte Tarpon Fly, and Orange & Yellow.

**Best tackle**

When pursuing larger, hundred-pound-and-up tarpon on the fly rod, the angler must go to the extremes of heavy fly fishing tackle: a nine- or ten-foot graphite or boron rod that casts eleven-, twelve-, or thirteen-weight line (weight forward), and heavy, indestructible saltwater fly reels as made by top manufacturers like Billy Pate, Fin-Nor, or Steve Abel. The reel should carry at least 250 yards of 30 lb.-test Dacron™ or Micron backing, and the fly line should be tied with a stout tippet between 8- and 16-lb. test (many anglers often add a shock tippet of 80-lb. test or thereabouts). Smaller tarpon require lighter weights, with eight- or ten-weight line and 8-lb. test tippets offering sufficient strength. When spinning or bait casting for the silver king (even if you do not expect to encounter larger tarpon), a slow-taper, stiff-butted seven-foot spinning or bait-casting rod fitted with at least 15- to 20 lb.-test line and a medium-sized saltwater spinning or bait-casting reel that can hold at least two hundred yards of line are essential. Where larger tarpon are a possibility, these weight classes must be upgraded if the angler is to have any hope of landing a fish.

*Typical tarpon flies. Fly rodding for tarpon requires patience, knowledge of local waters, superb casting ability, a strong upper body, and keen vision.*

# TUNA

*With each passing summer, there are fewer tuna in the waters over the Hudson Canyon. In the cloud-darkened depths, the bluefin move like shadows within a world of shadow. They do not behave as they once did—leaping forward at the surface and forming exploding lines from horizon to horizon to drive all the smaller fishes before them. Today they stay deep or cruise over the Continental Shelf with little fanfare. They seem to understand they are more the hunted than the hunters.*

—George Rieger, *Wanderer On My Native Shore*

© Sharkbait Productions

***Yellowfin aboard. The world record yellowfin caught on rod and reel weighed 388 pounds.***

Little did Charles Frederick Holder know when he caught the first recorded tuna on rod and reel in 1898 in Catalina, California, that he had unleashed one of the greatest passions in the history of outdoor sport—a passion for fish that would drive thousands of deep-sea anglers to spend millions of dollars with the determination of Ahab to pursue *Thunnus thynnus,* the strongest game fish alive.

As the years unfolded since Holder's catch, the weight of world-record bluefin crept higher and higher—from four and five hundred-pound catches to Zane Grey's 758-pound champion in 1924, to the first thousand-pound tuna boated in 1970 off Nova Scotia, to current world-record catches that tip Herculean scales at over twelve hundred and thirteen hundred pounds. The bluefin has captured the hearts of great anglers like Zane Grey and Ernest Hemingway, who boated the first tuna at Bimini, Bahamas, in 1935; Michael Lerner, who caught 642 bluefins over a lifetime; and Elwood K. Harry, president of the International Game Fish Association, who has boated a lifetime total of 612 big

© M. Timothy O'Keefe/Tom Stack & Associates

*Another prize yellowfin. Streamlined, fast, strong, and aggressive, large tuna can keep an angler engaged in battle for hours.*

tuna. As many first-time tuna anglers have discovered and remembered for days with aching shoulders and strained backs, catching a bluefin on rod and reel requires hours of exhausting muscle-busting work not unlike trying to haul a runaway car uphill.

Yellowfin, blackfin, and other smaller tuna (albacore, big eye, long tail, little tunny, skipjack), though extremely streamlined, fast, muscular and fond of deep, sounding dives against the hook as is the bluefin, offer more manageable sport. If caught on proper-sized tackle, both of these species will acquit themselves honorably in the ring but will not drag out the bout.

There are numerous tuna species caught with rod and reel but the bluefin, blackfin, and yellowfin are the most popular targets for anglers in North America.

The Atlantic and Pacific bonitos, close relatives of tuna, hunt and migrate in similar patterns. An easy find and very tough fight, the bonito is also favored by a good number of saltwater anglers in the Atlantic and Pacific.

Bonitos travel in temperate and tropical waters, always in schools. Adults range in size from five to twenty-five pounds, with the majority weighing in the low teens.

**Range**

Tuna are international citizens. The bluefin travels both sides of the Atlantic, the Pacific, and the Mediterranean. Bluefin have been caught off the African coast and found on the eastern Atlantic coast at various times of the year from the central Caribbean northward to Newfoundland. As Erwin A. Bauer points out in *The Saltwater Fisherman's Bible,* in 1958 a bluefin weighing thirty pounds was tagged at Guadalupe Island off Mexico; five years later it was caught 6,000 miles away in Japan, weighing over 240 pounds.

Every year bluefin travel a circular

*Smaller tuna like this albacore are excellent light-tackle sporting fish and can be released with little harm to the fish.*

migration that begins in spawning grounds that include the Gulf of Mexico, as well as the straits of Florida and waters between the Dominican Republic and the Bahamas. In late spring the bluefin migrate north through the Straits of Florida and past the Bahamas and Bermuda. By May the migrating bluefin are following the Gulf Stream far offshore past the southeastern U.S., Maryland, and Pennsylvania. They arrive at New Jersey, Montauk, Cape Cod, and Rhode Island through late June and early July.

By August, schools of hulking bluefins have settled in summering grounds off Nova Scotia, Newfoundland, and Prince Edward Island. Between August and September, these waters boast the richest concentration of bluefin on the Atlantic seaboard, feeding voraciously on butterfish, menhaden, and herring to fatten themselves for their long winter journeys. As the water cools, bluefin migrate south, dispersing widely through the south Atlantic, past Bermuda toward the Lesser Antilles. The bluefin continue south past Jamaica, Haiti, and the Venezuelan coast.

Yellowfin tuna are primarily a tropical water fish found off the Florida coast on both sides, in the Caribbean, throughout the Southern Pacific off Baja, and south past Mexico. They are also prevalent in Hawaiian waters. The blackfin tuna, favoring warmer waters, ranges from Cape Cod to Brazil.

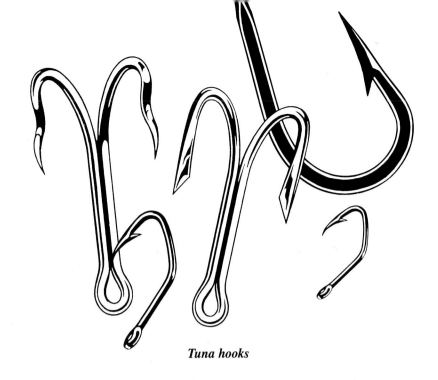
*Tuna hooks*

**Color**

The bluefin's body is dark blue on the back, brightening to a silver-white on the flanks and belly, and ghosted with a pale stripe of yellow at the pectoral fin.

Blackfin are handsome as well, painted on the back with dark, cobalt blue and wearing a bright butter-yellow stripe around the shimmering pale blue midsection. The yellowfin is the gaudiest tuna, boasting a blue-black back, silvery flanks striped with bright gold and yellow, a white spotted belly, and bright yellow fins.

**Identifying characteristics**

The tuna is shaped like a bullet (albeit a large one). Tuna fins fold down close against their bodies allowing them to move through the water with powerful strokes of their large, crescent-shaped tails at terrific speeds of thirty-five to forty mph. The blackfin is distinguished from other tuna by its very long pectoral fins and dark brown-black dorsal fins. Yellowfin tuna can be distinguished from blackfin by the black margins on their finlets as well as their overextended second dorsal and anal fins that may reach more than halfway to the tail.

**Size**

Bluefins often weigh more than 750 pounds. The world-record fish was taken off Nova Scotia in 1979, measuring thirteen feet long and weighing 1,496 pounds. Yellowfin average around forty or fifty pounds, but some heavier specimens are boated in the 175- to 200-pound range. The world record weighed 388½ pounds; it was caught near Mexico off San Benedicto Island. Although the blackfin are among the smallest tuna, they provide the liveliest sport on light tackle. They average around fifteen pounds although some blackies are caught at twenty-five or thirty pounds. They are the only tuna that can be lured close to a boat, approached, and managed on fly tackle.

**Spawning period**

Bluefin tuna spawn in the warm waters of the Gulf of Mexico and southern Atlantic and Caribbean during late spring. Blackfin reproduce in southern Florida waters, as well as the Bahamas and the Caribbean, from April to November. Yellowfin mate largely in spring and summer, seeking warm water. Tropical yellowfish will spawn year-round. Tuna hatchlings grow quickly, reaching sizes of ten pounds or more after eighteen months.

**Angling notes**

All tuna feast on pelagic baitfish, from mackerel and menhaden to herring and flying fish. The larger the tuna, the larger the individual fish it will pursue. Bluefin feed especially hard during their summer runs off the northeast coast, fattening for the long fall swim to

South America and the Gulf of Mexico's spawning grounds. Once hooked, tuna will head for the deep; a giant bluefin of more than three or four hundred pounds can tow a good-sized fishing boat for miles, and require hours of pumping and cranking (with the assistance of a skilled captain and a big boat engine) to bring the fish to the gaff.

Bluefin is big-game, big-tackle fishing with braided line, high-speed lures, huge boat reels, and glass rods. Chumming, linked to trolling of herring or other baitfish as the tuna are brought closer to the boat, is the primary angling method on professional tuna boats. Other captains will also trail large feathered trolling jigs to attract the tuna and, since many big fish hesitate to strike large baits, follow up by trolling smaller herring rigs that skip along the surface.

Favorite bluefin trolling areas include, during May and early June, Tuna Alley off Cat Cay and Bimini in the Bahamas; the open waters off Montauk and Rhode Island beginning in late June; and Canadian points around the Gulf of Saint Lawrence, off Prince Edward Island, and Nova Scotia in August and early September.

Yellowfin and blackfin can be taken on trolled strip baits or whole fish, feather jigs, and other trolling plugs. If a school is located, anglers can plug cast from the boat with medium-to-heavy-saltwater tackle and large spoons, tin squids, or silvery surface plugs.

The Atlantic and Pacific bonitos are pelagic, migratory predators that feed on smaller fish and squid near the surface. A variety of angling methods may be used, including surface trolling, casting, or if a school is at hand, live bait fishing or jigging. Angling decisions will depend on where the tuna are feeding and how many are schooling in the angling zone.

**Lures** Feathered jigs, plastic squid, and Konahead type big-game trolling lures, with size geared to the species pursued. Standard models include the Konahead, Moldcraft Swimmer, Arbogast Reto's Rig, and No Alibi trolling feathers.

**Bait** Strip bait (fish cut to rooster-tail along the ocean surface, imitating the action of flying fish), herring, mullet, and other baitfish should be rigged for fast top-water skipping and swimming.

**Best tackle** For bluefin, boat tackle in the 80 to 130 weight class offers the best percentages; lighter class tackle means longer battles and lost bluefin, the closer the hooked fish get to the eight hundred-pound class. Light saltwater and heavy fly tackle provide top challenge in catching blackfin and other smaller tuna. For the more cautious and less patient, medium-weight casting tackle will make shorter work of blackfin, and is absolutely necessary when casting to yellowfin. Trolling tackle is needed for larger yellowfin over seventy-five pounds; this is probably the safest choice when setting out for this species, which can run over two hundred pounds.

The bluefin tuna, believed by biblical scholars to be the fish that swallowed Jonah, has fascinated people for centuries and, should the bluefin and its angling nemesis survive, will fascinate them for centuries more.

# WAHOO

## (Pacific Kingfish)

*WAHOO*

**Range**
The wahoo is scattered throughout the tropical and warm waters of the Pacific and Atlantic, with heaviest concentrations off the Pacific coasts of Panama, Costa Rica, and Baja in California; Grand Cayman in the Atlantic; and near the Western Bahamas, and especially Bermuda, in spring and fall.

**Color**
The wahoo, one of the ocean's strongest and fastest saltwater game fish, is among the most beautiful of its inhabitants. Its back is an iridescent metallic blue that glitters in the sun, crossed by long, silvery blue-green bars that meet at the belly, which is a deep ivory.

**Identifying characteristics**
Although wahoo are very easy to identify, they are hard to come by. These cylindrical, streamlined predators look a great deal like their relatives the mackerel or small billfish. Their beaklike jaws, which are full of razor-sharp teeth, are suggestive of billfish jaws but lacking the bill. Both the upper and lower jaws are movable. The wahoo's first dorsal fin is waved, and the back is topped with a row of tunalike finlets. Electric blue-silver tiger stripes complete the highly recognizable picture.

**Size**
Wahoo travel in small pods of three to five adults, and they range in weight from fifty to seventy-five pounds, though fish over one hundred pounds are regularly caught. The all-tackle world record is a 149-pound fish caught off Cat Cay in the Bahamas.

**Spawning habits**
The wahoo spawn in the open ocean, laying millions of eggs that float until hatching—or until they are eaten by other fish.

**Angling notes**
The wahoo provides unparalleled open-water fishing excitement. This "cheetah of the sea" is capable of swimming at speeds over 50 mph, and can outswim and attack virtually any fish in the ocean. Wahoos hit baits and lures at top

© Allan Weltz

**The wahoo swims faster than any other pelagic gamefish: "The cheetah of the sea" reaches speeds of 50 miles per hour. Taming the wahoo's three hundred yard runs requires the service of a fighting chair.**

speed, stripping off hundreds of yards of monofilament in less than a minute. The angler who tries to slow down a wahoo run by "thumbing" the spool can burn off a quarter inch of flesh. The wahoo will test the angler with not one or two but three or four multi-hundred-yard runs complete with head-shaking jumps before its brilliant energy is spent.

Few saltwater anglers of any experience regret hooking up a wahoo, though they are relatively rare and often caught when anglers are pursuing billfish or other more widespread pelagic gamefish. Many are caught in the warm, shallow, blue water of the Keys as they migrate south in late fall and winter and on their way north in early spring. Cat Cay and the Tongue of the Ocean in the Bahamas host thousands of wahoo in spring and fall as do the waters off the shores of Bermuda where wahoo fishing is as good as anywhere in the world. From May to early June, wahoo run in the thousands over two southern Bermuda reef banks, Challenger Bank and Argus Bank. This fish-

ing holds steady throughout the summer, and chances of hooking and boating these predatory torpedos are excellent. Then as September rolls around, the major run begins and launches what can be considered the world's best wahoo fishing.

Unlimited numbers of wahoo patrol the banks until the end of October, when fishing traffic crisscrosses the area like cars moving through Times Square. Hookups are virtually guaranteed, and many hundred-plus-pounders are fought to the gaff.

**Lures** Those trolling feathers and plugs effective on other small pelagic gamefish such as dolphin and sailfish will take wahoo wherever they are found. Kona-heads, Tournament Tackle Islanders, Bubbleheads, Jelly Bellies, and Chummin' Squids are popular brands.

**Bait** Whole or strip-baited mackerel, mullet, ballyhoo, squid, and runner (when trolled at higher speeds) are the percentage takers for most pelagic gamefish, including wahoo.

**Best tackle** Boat tackle, including a fighting harness and fighting chair, is required for these fish of great strength, speed, and sharpness of tooth. Rod and reel should fall in the 5/0 and 6/0 class. Use test in the 30- to 50-lb. range and size 8/0 to 10/0 hooks, depending on how large the wahoo are running where you are fishing. The captain will have this information, as well as the tackle, if you rent out the boat for a half or full day. The jaws of the wahoo are filled with very sharp teeth. Unhook carefully—wire leaders are a must.

# WEAKFISH
## (Seatrout)

*WEAKFISH*

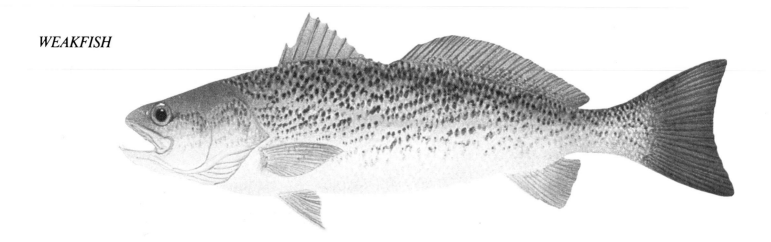

| | |
|---|---|
| **Range** | The weakfish (named for its tender mouth, which a hook will often tear) is common to most coastal waters of the middle and southern Atlantic, from Cape Cod to Virginia, North Carolina, Texas, and the Gulf of Mexico. Huge weakfish schools migrate north to the waters of New Jersey, New York, and Connecticut in summer, and shift south in winter where they can be found off the Gulf and Atlantic coasts of Florida. The white seabass is the Pacific Ocean cousin of the weakfish and the spotted seatrout. It can be found in the same waters as the weakfish, although it is more populous in southeastern U.S. coastal, tidal, and surf waters. |
| **Color** | Black back lightening to silver-white body with round black spots on back, upper flanks, and tail. |
| **Identifying characteristics** | Two large canine teeth in front of upper jaw, double dorsal fin. |
| **Size** | Most weakfish fall between two and three pounds although the dedicated weakfisher will pull in a five-pounder from time to time. |
| **Spawning period** | Weakfish spawn in spring, moving into warmer shallow estuaries and coastal zones. |
| **Angling notes** | Though not great fighters, weakfish are extremely available and compliant game fish. The weak will take shrimp, clams, crabs, and sliced baitfish from the bottom; it will strike jigs, spinners, flutters, spoons, and even bass plugs with complete lack of discretion. Since the weak is a good table fish, some anglers spend entire sum- |

© Tim Rhoad

**Weakfish can be angled after in bays and estuaries, and out of the waves and surf.**

mers making short work of it for backyard fish barbeques and other meals. Weakfishing is an excellent introduction to saltwater fishing for younger folks and novices. A very light saltwater spinning outfit, some light sinkers, live shrimp, a boxful of jigs and spinners—that's all it takes. Weakfish are often found in lagoons and flats around weeks and floating seaweed; they like hanging around pilings, piers, bridges, and other structures in tidal rivers and estuaries.

The seabass is not a bass, just as the seatrout is not a trout. Ranging throughout the eastern Pacific—largely between San Francisco and the Baja—the seabass frequents kelp beds and surf zones where it feeds on sardines, anchovies, and squid as well as small mackerels and other baitfish. Like its Atlantic cousins, the white seabass' mouth is soft, and easily torn by angling hooks. The seabass is a more popular angling target on the West Coast than its Yankee cousins back East. It can be caught with any variety of jigs, spoons, plugs, or baits. With West Coast anglers, however, drift and still fishing are the preferred angling methods. The seabass tends to prowl the bottom water layers for prey and shies away from the active surface feeding.

Jigs and live bait should be fished slowly and noisily (lots of tip action with your rod) over the bottom. Plugs and spinners should be retrieved slowly at middle depths. Weaks will often hit surface lures at night or early in the morning. Because the larger fish are nocturnal, night is the best time to catch a full dinner for four.

*The weak is beautiful in nature, and delicious at the table.*

*Weaks are often caught from piers and jetties. Jigs and baits should be fished noisily, near the bottom.*

# CALIFORNIA YELLOWTAIL

*CALIFORNIA YELLOWTAIL*

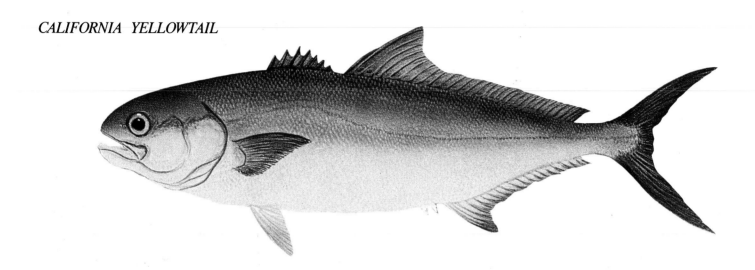

**Range**  Among the popular Pacific saltwater game fish, the yellowtail ranges from northwestern shores to blue waters of Mexico, but it is concentrated around southern California from Cabo San Lucas to the top of Baja, and in the northern regions of the Sea of Cortez. Yellowtail school and head into the southern Baja waters when the water temperature cools in fall. This is a prime southern California game fish, the all-out obsession of sport boats in the Baja, satisfying the three commandments of game fish satisfaction—fight, availability, and good eating.

**Color**  Long and streamlined, the yellowtail has a pointed snout; a brownish, olive, or blue-green back depending on habitat; greenish yellow dorsals and pectorals (sometimes flecked or barred with yellow on the margins); and a yellow tail—not surprisingly. The yellowtail's flanks are marked with a yellow stripe. A handsome fish indeed.

**Identifying characteristics**  The color of the California yellowtail's fins and bright yellow horizontal stripe are immediate clues to its origin. The yellowtail is closely related to the amberjack family; it can be hard to distinguish from the greater and Pacific amberjacks. However, the Pacific and greater amberjacks do not bear yellow stripes on their flanks; they are blackish silver in contrast to the brighter yellowtail. If identification is vital and you can't make an easy call, look under the gill flap. The yellowtails' gills have twenty-one to twenty-eight rakers while the greater amberjack's gills are made of only eleven to sixteen rakers.

**Size** Most southern California vacationers and casual anglers will put smaller fish on board—twenty pounds and under—as party boats tend to follow the big schools, which usually produce smaller fish. More selective and luckier yellowtail fanciers will catch fish in the thirty-to forty-pound range. The all-tackle world record for the California yellowtail is a 71-pound, 15-ounce huskie caught on trolling equipment in the Baja in 1979. The southern yellowtail, a very close cousin of the California breed, is a larger fish that is well distributed throughout the South Pacific. A number of world-record southern yellowtail have been caught at weights over one hundred pounds in New Zealand waters.

**Spawning period** Yellowtail spawn when waters are warmest between June and August in the open ocean.

**Angling notes** The yellowtail is one of the great sport fish of the masses, a fine and fighting big-game fish that schools in great numbers with lots of bottom-seeking power. Wide-ranging yellowtails will hit lures and baits on the bottom, the surface, near reefs, and on the open sea.

These are fast and well-muscled fish that give the Pacific angler a shoul-

*Yellowtail are a favorite of Pacific charter boats.*

© Howard Hall

**Yellowtail often travel in huge schools throughout Baja and the Sea of Cortez.**

der-throbbing full-value battle. Yellowtail will move from open water to coastal zones depending on food availability, and they will drive baitfish into the surf where the yellows can be caught on surf-casting tackle. They will move to the bottom to forage for crabs and shellfish, and sometimes they can be caught only on bottom-rigged tackle complete with sinkers, floats, and patience. The yellowtail is medium-tackle game that requires 20- to 30-lb. test on a large bait-casting reel or a 2/0 to 3/0 boat reel and a short, sturdy, stiff rod from 6.5 to 7 feet long. The yellowtail will pause before swallowing a bait: When you feel it strike on a trolled or bottom-drifted bait, wait three or four "beats" before striking.

Smaller yellowtail can be taken on heavy fly-fishing equipment: twelve-foot slow-taper rods, twelve-to-fourteen-weight fly line, wire leaders and large reels that hold at least three hundred yards of backing.

**Lures** Small white and blue plugs, feathers, squids, and large jigs are the usual choices. Yellowtail will hit smaller trolling lures at slow or fast speeds. When casting closer to shore from a stationary point, try larger lures to attract passing fish. As always when saltwater fishing, if a feeding school is located, virtually anything faintly resembling living food will be taken—a fork, cigar, candle, bare hook, or even a beer can.

**Bait** Use cut, strip, or whole baitfish when trolling, live or filleted fish or crushed crab or shrimp when bottom fishing near reefs.

**Flies** Large Mylar™ streamers and bucktails are required, tied with wire leader.

# Glossary

**Airbladder**    The membranous gas-filled organ in bony fish that regulates their swimming and holding depth in water. Also used by some fish to produce sound.

**Anadromous**    Referring to fish that live in salt water and migrate to fresh water to spawn.

**Alevin**    Hatchling salmonids living off their yolk sacs.

**Anterior**    Front section of fish.

**Barbel**    Thin whiskerlike tactile organ used by bottom-dwelling fish to locate food in sediment and sand.

**Basal**    Pertaining to or part of the base of an anatomical part.

**Benthic**    Occurring at or near the bottom of the ocean.

**Brackish**    Referring to rivers and other water bodies that contain both fresh and salt water; commonly includes tidal rivers, estuaries, tidal basins, and bays fed by freshwater rivers.

**Branchial**    Pertaining to the gills.

**Branchial arches**    The bony supports that connect the gill rakers and filaments to the fish's body.

**Cartilage**    Tough, white fibrous supportive tissue that cushions bones and composes the skeleton of sharks and rays.

**Catadromous**    Referring to fish that live in fresh water but migrate to salt water to spawn.

**Caudal fin**    The tail.

**Caudal peduncle**    The narrowing tail section or tail ''wrist'' between the fish's anal and tail fins.

**Cephalopod**    Member of a class of sea creatures that includes squids and octopi.

**Cetaceans**    Warm-blooded mammals of the sea, including dolphins and whales.

**Ciguatera**    A disease contracted by eating the flesh of certain tropical fish, including the barracuda, caused not by spoilage but peculiarities of diet.

**Crustacea**    Invertebrate sea creatures with rigid outer shells rather than skeletons, typically with segmented bodies and jointed limbs (crab, lobster).

**Cusp**    Small pointed projection at base of the tooth.

**Dorsal**    Relating to the back.

**Eutrophic**    Referring to a body of water enriched with organic matter and nutrients.

**Endemic**    Native to, indigenous.

**Falcate**    Sickle shaped.

**Finlet**    Small or vestigial fin.

**Fry**    Newly hatched fish after the yolk has been used up and active feeding begun.

**Fusiform**    Tapering toward each end; spindle shaped.

**Genus**  Taxonomic group of closely related, genetically similar fish of different species that may hybridize successfully, but are too similar to classify as family.

**Gills**  The breathing apparatus of fish.

**Gill filaments**  The thin, tissue-like structures on the outer edge of the gill arch that absorb oxygen from water.

**Gill rakers**  Series of bony structures on the inner edge of the gill that comb out food particles and prevent them from washing out the gill openings.

**Hermaphrodite**  An organism with male and female sexual organs.

**Homocercal**  Symmetrically formed.

**Ichthyology**  The science of fish behavior.

**Intromittent organ**  Organ for introducing sperm into body of female.

**Kype**  Prominent hooked jaw that develops in spawning male salmonids.

**Larva**  Newly hatched fish.

**Lateral**  Relating to the fish's flanks.

**Lateral line**  A strip of pores that run horizontally in various patterns and act as a sensory organ for fish, providing the "sense of distant touch."

**Lobe**  Rounded projection or subdivision of an exterior or interior piscine organ.

**Maxilla**  Bone of the fish's upper jaw.

**Median fins**  The unpaired fins, including dorsal, anal, and caudal.

**Migratory**  Refers to fish that travel long distances in fresh or salt water.

**Omnivorous**  Creature that feeds on wide variety of both plant and animal life.

**Opercle**  Large rectangular bone of the gill cover.

**Palatines**  Bones of the upper jaw on roof of the fish's mouth.

**Pelagic**  Refers to fish that live in the open waters of the ocean.

**Pelvic fins**  Paired fins on the lower part of a fish's body.

**Pharyngeal**  Region immediately behind the gills and anterior to the gut.

**Pharyngeal teeth**  Molars located on the bones of the pharynx.

**Piscivorous**  Refers to fish or mammals that feed primarily on fish.

**Plankton**  Microscopic plant and animal life that drift near the surface of the open water.

**Pyloric caeca**  Fingerlike extensions of the pylorus—the section of the intestinal tract following the stomach.

**Ray**  Supporting structures in the fins of fish.

**Redd**  Gravel spawning nest of salmonids.

**Reticulate**  Marked with a network or chain like pattern of lines.

**Riffle**  Shallow rapids in streams or rivers where the surface of water is broken.

**Rostrum**  Forward section of a fish's snout.

| | |
|---|---|
| **Sargassum** | Brown seaweed floating freely at sea that occurs in warm and tropical ocean waters. |
| **Serrations** | Sawlike edges on teeth. |
| **Snout** | Part of fish's head extending from the front margin of the eye to the anterior tip of the head. |
| **Spawn** | Act of reproduction by fish, involving release of eggs and sperm in the water. |
| **Species** | The fundamental taxonomic unit ranking after a genus and consisting of individuals that bear closest possible relationship to one another. |
| **Spiracle** | Small respiratory opening on back of the heads of some sharks and rays through which water is drawn into the gills. |
| **Substrate** | Bottom of a body of water. |
| **Truncate** | Referring to anatomical parts with straight rather than rounded edges. |
| **Turbid** | Water that is not clear. |
| **Ventral** | Pertaining to lower portion of fish's body. |
| **Vermiculations** | Wavy, wormlike markings found on backs of char and other salmonids. |
| **Villiform teeth** | Closely ranked, small and slender teeth that are crowded in such numbers that they cannot be easily counted. |
| **Vomer** | A bone in the middle of the roof of a fish's mouth. |

# Index

| UNIT | METRIC EQUIVALENT |
|------|-------------------|
| mile | 1.609 kilometers |
| yard | 0.9144 meters |
| foot | 30.48 centimeters |
| inch | 2.54 centimeters |
| ton | 0.907 metric ton |
| pound | 0.454 kilogram |
| ounce | 28.350 grams |

$°F - 32 \times 5 \div 9 = °C$

**Silhouetted photographs**

Courtesy Luhr-Jensen: 46, 48
Courtesy Daiwa Corporation: 85, 100
Courtesy Orvis: 91
Courtesy Eagle Claw Fishing Tackle/Wright &
 McGill Co.: 121, 127